Welten / Worlds

Worlds

Gertrud Kolmar

translated by

philip kuhn
&
ruth von zimmermann

Shearsman Books

First published in the United Kingdom in 2012 by
Shearsman Books
50 Westons Hill Drive
Emersons Green, Bristol BS16 7DF

Shearsman Books Ltd Registered Office
30–31 St. James Place, Mangotsfield, Bristol BS16 9JB
(this address not for correspondence)

http://www.shearsman.com/

ISBN 978-1-84861-198-6

Acknowledgements
Julian Marshall for introducing us to Kolmar;

Suhrkamp Verlag, Berlin, for permission to publish our translation of
Welten;

Wallstein Verlag for permission to use the text of *Welten* in Regina
Nörtemann's critical edition, *Gertrud Kolmar, Das lyrische Werk, Band 2:
Gedichte 1927–1937* (Göttingen, 2003);

Tony Frazer for publishing earlier versions of 'Borzoi', 'The Angel
in the Forest' & 'The Urals', in *Shearsman* 83 & 84 (2010);

Harry Guest for his most helpful & insightful responses,

& last, but not least, Regina Nörtemann for her support, and her
generous reading and perceptive commenting upon these
translations whilst they were still in manuscript.

CONTENTS

PROLOGUE

Regina Nörtemann

When I first heard Philip Kuhn reading some of the Gertrud Kolmar poems that he and Ruth von Zimmermann had translated into English I had a strange experience because I could hear the original German simultaneously: its melody, its rhythm and force of imagery. All these elements seemed to co-exist in the two languages at the same time.

As I understand the difficulties of translating poetry I was curious to know how Ruth and Philip had worked together on this project and managed to *English* Kolmar's poetical voice without losing its uniqueness. It was, therefore, a great honour and pleasure to read their *congenial* translation of *Welten* whilst it was still in manuscript.

This book is a collaboration between an English poet, whose Jewish roots are in Bamberg and whose own poetry abounds in metaphors and alliterations, and a musician and dance-teacher whose mother-tongue is German but who has been living in England for a long time. I hope that their work receives the recognition it deserves.

Gertrud Kolmar once wrote that she knew that she was a poet. But she also loved to say that in her youth she wanted to become a dancer.

Now look at, read and listen to her *suite* of worlds in two languages.

SOME BRIEF COMMENTS ON
GERTRUD KOLMAR'S LIFE AND WORKS

philip kuhn

Gertrud Käthe Chodziesner was born on 10 December 1894 into an assimilated Berlin Jewish family.[1] Her father Ludwig was a successful criminal lawyer and her mother Elise (née Schönflies) was Walter Benjamin's aunt. Gertrud had three younger siblings, Margot (b.1897), Georg (b.1900) and Hilde (b.1905). On leaving school she trained as a teacher and then worked in a nursery school. In 1915 she had an ill-fated love affair with Karl Jodl, a non-Jewish army officer, which led to an abortion and subsequent suicide attempt. Having studied Russian, English and French, she was employed, in 1917, as a letter censor in a prisoner-of-war camp near Spandau. Following the Armistice she worked in Berlin as a private tutor and governess before moving to Hamburg in 1927. In the autumn of that year she attended a vacation course at Dijon University and took the opportunity to visit Paris. Shortly after she returned to Germany, in March 1928, her mother fell ill and then following her mother's death, in March 1930, Gertrud started working as her father's secretary and also assumed full-time responsibilities for the family household which was now situated in Finkenkrug (Falkensee), an "idyllic" rural suburb of Berlin.

After Hitler seized power in early 1933 there followed a barrage of anti-Semitic decrees which, over the next five years, placed German Jews under ever-tightening restrictions. Unlike her siblings Gertrud chose to remain in Germany, or perhaps more specifically, she felt unable to abandon her father. Following the 1938 *Novemberpogrom* (the so-called *Kristallnacht*) Ludwig was forced to sell the family home, where he had been living since 1923, and re-locate, with his daughter, to a "Jewish" apartment in Berlin. Before long other families were billeted with them so that eventually Gertrud had to live with "strangers who have taken possession of everything that is mine ... and nothing belongs to me anymore."[2] Like thousands of other Jews, the Chodziesners were now trapped inside Germany, their rights systematically curtailed and their freedom of movement confined to an ever-diminishing radius. In July 1941, at the age of 47, Gertrud was conscripted to a weapons' factory in Lichtenberg and then, some fourteen months later, re-assigned to work in a factory in Charlottenburg. In September 1942 her father was deported to Theresienstadt where he died some five months later. Then on 27 February 1943 Gertrud was arrested in the so-called *Fabrikaktion* and 'deported' to Auschwitz on the 2nd March transport. There is no record of what happened to her after she was forced onto the train but if she had survived that nightmare journey east she would have been "selected" on arrival, and murdered in the gas ovens.

Gertrud's first publication, a small collection of poems, appeared in 1917 and was initiated by her father. She chose Kolmar as her *nom de plume* because, as she later explained, it was the name the Germans had used, in 1874, when they "re-christened" Chodziez, the Polish town in Poznán which was "the place of origin of the Chodziesner family".[3] It is generally accepted that Kolmar's first book, and the subsequent poems she wrote around 1920, were nothing special.[4] But then something happened in 1927—around the time she travelled to France—because over the next thirteen years she produced a significant body of work: two prose narratives, *Die jüdische Mutter* [The Jewish Mother (1931)] and *Susanna* (1940): the drama *Cécile Renault* (1935), the dramatic legend *Nacht* [Night (1938)], the historical study of Robespierre, *Das Bildnis Robespierres* (1933), and the ninety-five letters and postcards which she wrote to her sister and niece, Hilde and Sabine Wenzel, after the Wenzel family escaped into Switzerland in September 1938. But perhaps most important of all were the ten poetry cycles: *Das preußische Wappenbuch* [Prussian Coats of Arms Book], *Weibliches Bildnis* [Female Portraits], *Tierträume* [Animal Dreams], *Mein Kind* [My Child] and *Bild der Rose* [Image of the Rose] which were all written between 1927 and 1932. These were followed by *Das Wort der Stummen* [The Word of the Mute (1933)] , *Robespierre* (1934), *Sieben Gedichte aus "German Sea" von Helen Lodgers* (1934), *Vier religiöse Gedichte* [Four Religious Poems (1937)] and *Welten* [Worlds] which she wrote between 17 August and 20 December 1937 and which contains her last extant poems.

Kolmar's work remained virtually unknown and largely unpublished during her life-time and has only survived because of the care and dedication of her sister and brother-in-law, Hilde and Peter Wenzel, her friend and cousin Sus(anne) Jung and Hilde Benjamin, the wife of her cousin Georg. Although Peter Wenzel persuaded *Suhrkamp* to publish *Welten* as early as 1947 and Hermann Kasack edited a collection of her *lyrische Werk* in 1955 Kolmar's obscurity continued well into the post-war period. Interest in her life and work began to grow in the 1990s but it was not until 2003, with the publication of Regina Nörtemann's Three Volume Critical Edition, that scholars and enthusiasts had, for the first time, a solid and reliable text of Kolmar's entire *lyrische Werk*. Since then interest in Kolmar's writings has spread beyond the German-speaking world and her work is now translated, or in the process of being translated, into Hungarian, Russian, Italian, Polish, French, Spanish, and Ukrainian.

If Kolmar is still a relatively esoteric figure in twentieth century German Literature she remains virtually unknown in the English speaking world. During the course of our researches we have only identified some twenty-five English language publications on Kolmar in the sixty-six year period since the end of the War. English translations have been even sparser. Two Kolmar poems, translated by Christopher Middleton, appeared in *Modern German Poetry*, the anthology which Middleton co-edited with Michael Hamburger in 1962. Eight years later Magpie Press published David Kipp's *Selected Poems of Gertrud Kolmar* (1970), a chapbook of twenty-eight translations drawn from Friedhelm Kemp's 1960 edition of *Das Lyrische Werk*.

In 1975 non-German English speakers were offered their first opportunity to gain a sense of the breadth and depth of Kolmar's poetic *oeuvre* with the publication of Henry Smith's *Dark Soliloquy*. Smith's dual text contains fifty-three translations selected from five of the ten cycles and also includes his long and informative biographical essay. Although Smith's book received positive reviews it appears to have generated little interest because we have been unable to find any further Kolmar translations until 1995 when Millennium published Elizabeth Spencer's *The Shimmering Crystal*, a dual text chapbook containing fourteen translations drawn from the 1955 Kasack edition. Grimm and Hunt included only one Kolmar poem in their *German 20th Century Poetry* (2001) but this turns out to be one of Smith's 1975 translations. Eavan Boland included only one Kolmar translation in her *After Every War* (2004). As for Kolmar's prose; her two novellas, *A Jewish Mother from Berlin* and *Susanna*, were published in America in a single-volume translation in 1997, whilst *My Gaze Is Turned Inward*, a translation of Kolmar's letters (1934–1943) was published in 2004. This book also contains a short afterword by Johanna Woltmann, the noted Kolmar scholar, and an interesting preface including translations of seven Kolmar poems by the book's translator Brigitte Goldstein.[5]

It might be worth speculating why Kolmar's writings have attracted this degree of neglect. One possible answer, hinted at by Ruth Schwertfeger, is that a series of significant manuscripts, written through "Auschwitz", have effectively eclipsed works written in the decade that predated that "year zero".[6] It is quite likely, therefore, that Kolmar's work has been obscured by that small but significant body of Jewish writers who lived through the *Shoah* (the Holocaust) and engraved their anguished experiences in ink. There were those who escaped Germany in time, like Nelly Sachs, or Else Lasker-Schüler. There were those who "survived", like Rose Ausländer, Paul Celan, Piotr Rawicz[7] and Primo Levi.[8] And then there was Miklós Radnóti who appeared *out of the ashes* after a notebook of his poems was discovered in his raincoat pocket when his body was exhumed from a mass grave one year after the end of the war.[9] All this suggests that because Kolmar's writings were cut short on the very eve of the *Shoah* they have been consigned to some preconceived cultural no-man's land between Weimar (1919–1933) and "Auschwitz". This fact alone may well have persuaded many potential Kolmar readers to assume that her writings offered little or nothing of consequence. We hope that this book will argue otherwise.

Once the two of us had decided upon a Kolmar poetry collaboration we instinctively favoured working with an entire cycle rather than a random selection of poems.[10] *Welten* was the obvious choice because it is relatively short, at least compared to some of Kolmar's other cycles—*Weibliches Bildnis*, for example, comprises seventy-five poems. This was important because it was to be our first attempt at translating German poems into English. But there was also another consideration: *Welten* does not have the strict meter and regular rhyme schemes that are so characteristic of Kolmar's other cycles. This meant that we could side-step all those potentially intractable conundrums that would inevitably have arisen had we tried to twist Kolmar's metres and rhymes into English. This is not to suggest that *Welten* is somehow free from technical difficulties but simply to acknowledge that neither of us felt inclined, let alone competent enough, to deal with such formal verse forms. And yet we still had our work cut-out not only trying to convey something of Kolmar's unique lyrical style but also wondering how best to deal with her "wunderbares verbarium"[11]—her strange, uncanny vocabulary.

Kolmar's *Worlds* are inhabited by many diverse and mysterious beings that throb just "beneath the surface of things."[12] Some of those *Worlds* are populated by exotic plants, magical animals, strange "peoples"—real or imagined: some are colonised by phantoms and ghosts, or by seductive lovers, at first tender and amorous then, suddenly, menacing. Others are visited by semi-mystical beings or perhaps by *revenants* returned so that they might entwine themselves around familiars or anthropomorphic shades already pulsating in sensual, semi-ritual dance.

In this translation we have striven to find consistent workable English equivalents that will not just capture the literal meanings of each poem but also suggest something of the architectonics of the cycle as a whole. To try and define the shape and timbre of Kolmar's language without domesticating its strange and alien tone. To join together her sense, sensuousness and song and thereby re-fashion *Welten* so that English readers might hear Kolmar's unique poetic voice beckoning from beyond the chasms of language and time.

NOTES

1   Biographical information is drawn mainly from R. Nörtemann (ed.), *Gertrud Kolmar, Das lyrische Werk: Anhang und Kommentar*, Göttingen: Wallstein Verlag, 2003, Vol. 3, pp.397f.

2   Gertrud Kolmar, *My Gaze is Turned Inward: Letters, 1934–1943*, trans. Brigitte M. Goldstein, Evanston, IL: Northwestern University Press, 2004, p.135.

3   Johanna Woltmann, in *ibid*, p.166.

4   These and other early poems can be found in ed. Nörtemann, *op. cit.*, *Frühe Gedichte* Vol. 1.

5   Kolmar, *op. cit.* This volume includes several letters to miscellaneous others including Jacob Picard and her cousin Walter Benjamin.

6   R. Schwertfeger, 'Jewish Writing in German Continues in Theresienstadt and Beyond', in S. L. Gilman & J. Zipes, *Yale Companion to Jewish Writing and Thought in German Culture, 1096–1996*, New Haven, CT: Yale University Press, 1997, p.615.

7   Piotr Rawicz was in Auschwitz for more than two years. See A. Rudolf, *Engraved in Flesh: Piotr Rawicz and his novel Blood from the Sky*, London: Menard Press, 2007.

8   Primo Levi was also a survivor of Auschwitz.

9   Miklós Radnoti was sent to a forced labour camp in occupied Serbia. He was executed on 9 November 1944 during a forced march back into Hungary.

10   A more detailed account of our collaboration can be found in our essay, 'On Translating 'Welten' in Chryssoula Kambas and Marion Brandt (eds.), *'Sand in den Schuhen Kommender'. Gertrud Kolmars Werk im Dialog*, Göttingen: Wallstein Verlag, 2012, pp.265–275

11   This concept is Vera Viehöver's, for which see her essay 'Altfränkisch duftend wie Levkojenblüten' in Gertrud Kolmars wunderbares Verbarium, *ibid*, pp. 251–263.

12   H. A, Smith, *Dark Soliloquy: The Selected Poems of Gertrud Kolmar*, New York: Continuum, 1975, p.11

Our thanks to Anthony Rudolf and Richard Berengarten for their invaluable comments during the drafting of this essay.

Die Mergui-Inseln

Die Mergui-Inseln sind Laich.
Hingesamt vor den Schenkel des Frosches,
Der, blaues Birma, gelbes Siam, grünes Annam,
Hockt und rudert, den Schwimmfuß Malakka in chinesische
    Fluten stößt.
Nein.
Meine Mergui-Inseln baden nicht singend im indischen Meere.
Sie tauchen aus Nachtsee schweigsam in stetig tagloses
    Dämmer empor,
Kuppig, schwarzgrün bezottelt,
Widerriste ungeheurer Büffel, die in Meertiefe bräunlichen
    Tang durchweiden.
Ihre Nüster kocht Schaum.
Ihre Flanke rauscht Finsternis. Fahl schwelendes
    Wetterleuchten
Zittert aus dem gebogenen Horn.
Verglostet …

Unter dornigem Struppwerk des Kamms
Ducken, mit Pferdshaaren, fluglose Vögel sich, die noch kein
    Forscher erkannt hat.
Von steiniger Lichtung
Starrt mondgoldnes Auge schiefergrauer reglos gewundener
    Schlange in ewigen Abend auf.

Aber in Kalksteinhöhlen,
Deren Wände zerfressen von Wellenschnauzen, zernagt sind
    von Tropfenzähnen,

The Mergui Islands

The Mergui Islands[1] are spawn.
Seeded there in front of the thigh of the frog,
Which, blue Burma, yellow Siam, green Annam[2]
Squats and paddles, pushing the webbed foot Malacca
       into Chinese waters.
No.
My Mergui Islands do not swim, singing in the Indian Ocean.
They rise upwards silently out of night sea into steady
       dayless half-light,
Humped, matted black-green,
Ridged backs of monstrous buffaloes, which graze through
       the brownish seaweed in the depth of the sea.
Their nostril boils foam.
Their flank whooshes darkness. Pale smouldering
       sheet lightning
Trembles out of the inflected horn.
Fades away ...

Under thorny scrubs of the crest
Cower flightless birds with horse hair which no researcher
       has yet recognised.
From stony clearing
Golden moon eye of motionlessly coiled slate grey serpent
       stares towards everlasting evening.

But in limestone caverns,
Whose walls are eaten through by wave-mouths,
       gnawed through by teeth drips,

---

[1] The Mergui or Myeik islands are a group of hundreds or thousands of
smaller and bigger green jewels in the Andaman Sea, located at the southern
most part of Myanmar, formerly Burma.
[2] A French protectorate encompassing the central region of Vietnam.

Feiern Meerechsen in malachitgrünem Brautschmuck
    brünstige Vermählungen,
Kröpft schwarzer Geier mit kahlem, blaurotem Antlitz
    scharlachflossigen Fisch,
Huschen aus Löchern dunkle Schwalben, erdbraun
    beschwingt, mit veilchendüsteren Brüsten,
Blühn nelken- und safranfarb Blumentiere, atmen schon
    Beute, fächeln mit Fangarmen hin,
Rollt eine große Schnecke sich in den pantherfleckigen
    porzellanenen Mantel ein.
Und schlummert.

Schiffe wurden verweht.
Verweht … zerrissen … Planken treiben, Fetzen der Welt,
Die den Meißel des Werkers trägt und des Schreibenden Stift
    und den Pflug und Kaufmanns Gewicht und Waage,
Tausend hastende Räder, tausend haspelnde Worte
Und das Geld. —Hier kauert im Ungestirnten
Stummes Zwielicht,
Fern sanfter Mondklage, glühenden, blitzenden Sonnengesängen.
Land träumt, ummurmelt von salzig triefenden Lefzen
    uralter Amme.
Dumpf weißliches Glimmen sinnt.
Nur Tier und Pflanze.
Seltsame Grottenratte, die graulich gesprenkeltes,
    türkisfarbes Ei bebrütet,
Schlafstrauch, des tintige Beeren
Den Esser für eines Jahrs Hingang in Druseln lullen—doch
    niemand pflückt sie geschäftig …
Stille.
Sein noch ohne Tun.

Wo Schlinggerank klammernd mit mageren Armen schuppige
    Zwergstämme würgt,
Unter Akaziengefieder
Bricht aus tiefgrüner Blattscheide einsame Frucht hervor,
Lang und gerundet, steil in nackter, fleischiger Röte
    schwellend.

Ocean lizards in malachite-green bridal ornaments
    celebrate lustful marriages,
Black vulture with bald blue-red countenance gorges
    scarlet finned fish,
Dark swallows dart out of cavities, earth brown winged,
    with dusky violet breasts,
Carnation and saffron coloured animal flowers blossom, already
    breathing their prey, fanning with tentacles,
A great snail rolls itself into the panther spotted
    porcelain cloak.
And slumbers.

Ships were blown away.
Blown away ... torn ... Planks drift, scraps of the world,
Which carries the chisel of the worker and the crayon of the writer
    and the plough, and the weight and scales of the merchant,
A thousand rushing wheels, a thousand spluttering words
And the money. —Here mute twilight
Cowers in the starless space,
Far from gentle moon lament, from glowing, flashing sun songs.
Land dreams surrounded by the murmur of the salty
    dripping jowls of ancient wet-nurse.
Muffled white-ish glint muses.
Only animal and plant.
Strange grotto rat which incubates grey speckled
    turquoise-coloured egg,
Sleeping shrub, whose inky berries
Lull the eater into a doze for the passing of a year—
    but nobody plucks them busily ...
Silence.
Being yet without doing.

Where vines, clinging with emaciated arms, throttle flaking
    dwarf stems,
Under acacia plumage,
From the deep green leaf-sheath, a solitary fruit bursts forth
Long and rounded, upright swelling in naked
    fleshy redness.

Sie wartet,
Bis Lippen leisen, schwüleren Hauches
Flüsternd durch Dickicht tasten, rühren, schauern,
    umhüllen:
Sie bebt
Und die im Fruchtfleisch verborgenen Stränge gießen
    zeugenden Samen aus.

It waits,
Till the lips of a faint, more sultry breeze
Whispering through the thicket, feel, stir, shudder,
    shroud:
It quivers,
And skeins concealed in the flesh of the fruit pour out
    fertilising seed.

Sehnsucht

Ich denke dein.
Immer denke ich dein.
Menschen sprachen zu mir, doch ich achtet' es nicht.
Ich sah in des Abendhimmels tiefes Chinesenblau, daran der
    Mond als runde gelbe Laterne hing,
Und sann einem anderen Monde, dem deinen, nach,
Der dir glänzender Schild eines ionischen Helden vielleicht
    oder sanfter goldener Diskus eines erhabenen Werfers wurde.
Im Winkel der Stube saß ich dann ohne Lampenlicht,
    tagmüde, verhüllt, ganz dem Dunkel gegeben,
Die Hände lagen im Schoß, Augen fielen mir zu,
Doch auf die innere Wand der Lider war klein und unscharf
    dein Bild gemalt.
Unter Gestirnen schritt ich an stilleren Gärten, den
    Schattenrissen der Kiefern, flacher, verstummter
    Häuser, steiler Giebel vorbei
Unter weichem düsteren Mantel, den nur zuweilen
    Radknirschen griff, Eulenschrei zerrte,
Und redete schweigend von dir, Geliebter, dem lautlosen,
    dem weißen mandeläugigen Hunde, den ich geleitete.

Verschlungene, in ewigen Meeren ertrunkene Nächte!
Da meine Hand in den Flaum deiner Brust sich bettete zum
    Schlummer,
Da unsere Atemzüge sich mischten zu köstlichem Wein, den
    wir in Rosenquarzschale darboten unserer Herrin, der Liebe,
Da in Gebirgen der Finsternis die Druse uns wuchs und
    reifte, Hohlfrucht aus Bergkristallen und fliedernen Amethysten,
Da die Zärtlichkeit unserer Arme Feuertulpen und
    porzellanblaue Hyazinthen aus welligen, weiten, ins
    Morgengraun reichenden Schollen rief,
Da, auf gewundenem Stengel spielend, die halberschlossene
    Knospe des Mohns wie Natter blutrot über uns züngelte,

Yearning

I think of you,
I think of you always.
People spoke to me, but I didn't take heed.
I looked into the deep Chinese blue of the evening sky from which
    the moon hung as a round yellow lantern,
And mused upon another moon, yours,
Which became for you the dazzling shield of an Ionian hero, maybe,
    or the soft golden discus of an exalted thrower.
In the corner of the room I sat then without lamplight,
    day weary, veiled, given entirely to the darkness,
The hands lay in the lap, my eyes fell shut.
But onto the inner septum of the eyelids was painted your picture
    small and blurred.
Under stars I strode past quieter gardens, the
    silhouettes of pine trees, shallow silenced
    houses, steep gables,
Under soft dusky cloak, which was only occasionally
    seized by wheel grinding, tugged by owl screech,
And I talked silently of you, beloved, to the noiseless,
    to the white almond-eyed dog, which I led.

Engulfed nights, drowned in everlasting seas!
When my hand bedded itself in the down of your chest to
    slumber,
When our breaths blended into an exquisite wine, which
    we offered to our Goddess, Love, in a rose quartz bowl,
When in the mountains of darkness the druse grew and ripened
    for us, hollow fruit of rock crystals and lilac amethysts,
When the tenderness of our arms called fiery tulips and
    porcelain blue hyacinths from wide undulating earth
    reaching into dawn,
When, playing on twisted stem, the half opened
    bud of the poppy, like a viper, flicked blood-red over us,

Des Ostens Balsam- und Zimmetbäume mit zitterndem
    Laube um unser Lager sich hoben
Und purpurne Weberfinken unserer Munde Hauch in
    schwebende Nester verflochten. —
Wann wieder werden wir in des Geheimnisses Wälder fliehn,
    die, undurchdringlich, Hinde und Hirsch vor dem
    Verfolger schützen?
Wann wieder wird mein Leib deinen hungrig bittenden
    Händen weißes duftendes Brot, wird meines Mundes
    gespaltene Frucht deinen dürstenden Lippen süß sein?
Wann wieder werden wir uns begegnen?
Innige Worte gleich Samen von Würzkraut und
    Sommerblumen verstreun
Und beglückter verstummen, um nur die singenden Quellen
    unseres Blutes zu hören?
(Fühlst du, Geliebter, mein kleines horchendes Ohr, ruhend
    an deinem Herzen?)
Wann wieder werden im Nachen wir gleiten unter
    zitronfarbem Segel,
Von silbrig beschäumter, tanzender Woge selig gewiegt,
Vorüber an Palmen, die grüner Turban schmückt wie
    den Sproß des Propheten,
Den Saumriffen ferner Inseln entgegen, Korallenbänken,
    an denen du scheitern willst?
Wann wieder, Geliebter … wann wieder … ? …

Nun sintert mein Weg
Durch Ödnis. Dorn ritzt den Fuß.
Bäche, frische, erquickende Wasser, murmeln; aber ich finde
    sie nicht.
Datteln schwellen, die ich nicht koste. Meine
    verschmachtende Seele
Flüstert ein Wort nur, dies einzige:
»Komm …«
O komm …

When balsa and cinnamon trees of the east lifted themselves
    around our bed with quivering leaves
And crimson weaver finches intertwined our mouth's breath into
    floating nests. —
When will we flee again into the forests of the secret,
    which, impenetrable, shelter hind and deer from the
    pursuer?
When will my body be again white fragrant bread
    for your hungry beseeching hands, the split fruit of my mouth
    be sweet to your thirsting lips?
When will we meet each other again?
Strew heartfelt words like seeds of aromatic herbs and
    summer flowers
And fall silent, happier, so as to hear only the singing sources
    of our blood?
(Beloved, do you feel my small listening ear
    resting on your heart?)
When will we glide again in the barque under
    lemon coloured sail,
Rocked blissfully by silver foamed dancing wave,
Past palms adorned by a green turban, like
    the scion of the prophet,
Towards the fringe reefs of distant islands, coral reefs,
    on which you want to founder?
When again, beloved, ... when again ...?...

Now my path sinters
Through wasteland. Thorn scratches the foot.
Streams, cool, refreshing waters, murmur; but I don't find
    them.
Dates swell, which I don't taste. My
    starving soul
Mutters one word only, this one:
"Come ..."
Oh come ...

Das Einhorn

Der Pfauen Pracht,
Blau, grün und gülden, blühte in Dämmerung
Tropischer Wipfelwirrnis, und graue Affen
Fletschten und zankten, hangelten, tummelten, balgten sich
    im Geschlinge.
Der große Tiger, geduckt, zuckte die Kralle, starrte, verhielt,
Als das stumme seltsame Wild durch seine indischen Wälder
    floh,
Westwärts zum Meere.

Das Einhorn.

Seine Hufe schlugen die Flut
Leicht, nur spielend. Wogen bäumten sich
Übermütig,
Und es lief mit der wiehernd springenden, jagenden
    silbermähnigen Herde.
Über ihnen
Schrieb Flug schwarzer Störche eilige Rätselzeichen an den
    Himmel Arabiens,
Der mit sinkender Sonne eine Fruchtschale bot:
Gelbe Birnen, gerötete Äpfel,
Pfirsich, Orange und prangende Trauben,
Scheiben reifer Melone.
Schwarze Felsen glommen im Untergange,
Amethystene Burgen,
Weiße glühten, verzauberte Schlösser aus Karneol und Topas.

Spät hingen Rosennebel über den taubenfarb dunkelnden
    Wassern der Bucht.

Das Einhorn.

The Unicorn

The peacocks' splendour
Blue, green and golden, blossomed in the dusk
Of dense tropical tree-tops, and grey monkeys
Snarled and squabbled, climbed, romped, tussled
    in the tendrils.
The great tiger, crouching, flexed the claw, stared, held back
As the mute, strange animal fled through his Indian
    forests,
Westwards towards the sea.

The Unicorn.

His hooves pounded the waters
Lightly, only playing. Waves bucked
Boisterously,
And he ran with the whinnying, jumping, chasing
    silver-maned herd.
Above them
A flight of black storks wrote hurried enigmatic signs
    onto the Arabian sky
Which, with the setting sun, offered a fruit bowl:
Yellow pears, reddened apples,
Peach, orange and resplendent grapes,
Segments of ripe melon.
Black rocks glimmered in its setting,
Amethyst castles,
White ones glowed, enchanted palaces of cornelian and topaz.

Later roseate mists hovered over the dove coloured darkening
    waters of the bay.

The Unicorn.

Seine Hufe wirbelten Sand,
Der lautlos stäubte. Es sah
Einsame Städte, bleich, mit Kuppel und Minarett und den
    Steinen der Leichenfelder
Schweigend unter dem klingenden Monde.
Es sah
Trümmer, verlassene Stätten, nur von Geistern behaust, in
    funkelnder Finsternis
Unter kalten Gestirnen.
Einmal lockte der Wüstenkauz,
Und im Fernen heulten Schakale klagend;
Hyänen lachten.
Am Eingang des Zeltes unter der Dattelpalme
Hob das weiße syrische Dromedar träumend den kleinen
    Kopf, und seine Glocke tönte.

Vorüber das Einhorn, vorüber.

Denn seine leichten, flüchtigen Füße kamen weit her aus
    dem Goldlande Ophir,
Und aus seinen Augen glitzerten Blicke der Schlangen, die
    des Beschwörers Flöte aus Körben tauchen, gaukeln
    und tanzen heißt,
Doch das steile Horn seiner Stirnmitte goß sanfteres Licht,
    milchig schimmerndes,
Über die nackten Hände und weich umschleierten Brüste
    der Frau,
Die da stand
Zwischen Mannasträuchern.

Ihr Gruß:
Demut
Und der stille Glanz tiefer, wartender Augen
Und ein Hauchen, leise quellendes Murmeln des Mundes. —
    Brunnen in Nacht.

His hooves swirled sand,
Which powdered without sound. He saw
Lonely cities, pale, with dome and minaret and the
    stones of burial grounds
Silent under the sounding moon.
He saw
Ruins, abandoned sites, only inhabited by ghosts, in
    sparkling darkness
Under cold stars.
Once the desert screech-owl beckoned
And in the far-off jackals howled mournfully;
Hyenas laughed.
By the entrance to the tent under the date palm
The white Syrian dromedary dreamily lifted the little
    head, and its bell sounded.

Gone by, the unicorn has gone by.

Because his light, fleeting feet came from far away,
    out of Ophir, the land of gold,
And out of his eyes glittered the look of serpents, which
    the charmer's flute bids emerge out of the basket,
    pulsating and dancing,
Yet the upright horn of his mid-forehead poured softer light,
    milky shimmering,
Over the naked hands and the softly veiled breasts
    of the woman,
Who stood there
Between manna-bushes.

Her greeting:
Humility
And the still lustre of deep, waiting eyes
And a breath, faintly welling murmur of the mouth. —
    Fountains in night.

Dienen

Der du die Stoffe bindest und löst, kältest und glühst, sie
    schwächst und bekräftigst,
Der du Säuren reizt, Erze peinigst, geheime Mischung in
    Kapseln birgst, in Röhren und Tiegeln braust,
Wenngleich nicht der Alkahest noch der weiße oder der rote
    Löwe ist, was du siedest,
Adept einer Alchimie, die mir fremd und wunderbar dünkt;
Herr du des Feuers, das du in ehernem Käfig bändigst, das
    nun kriechend sich duckt wie ein sprungbereit lauerndes
    Raubtier,
Einst schnellte, die Stäbe zertrümmerte, wütende Krallen um
    deine Glieder schlug (o, mir bangt, wenn ich's denke!):
Ich will eine andere Flamme locken, milde, gezähmte Glut,
    die mir auf dem Herde schmeichelt und schnurrt und
    spielt wie ein häusliches Kätzchen;
Denn bunte Speisen will ich bereiten, ein kleines Mahl, das
    dich freuen soll,
Wenn du müde und doch mit Lächeln in meine dämmernden
    Räume kehrst.
Was scheltet ihr mich?
Was spottet ihr mein?
Weil meine Welt flach ist, wenig Schritt im Geviert,
    engumbaut,
Voll ruhmlos kleinlicher Dinge, geringfügiger Verrichtungen,
Erfüllt vom Klappern der Näpfe, Brodeln der Töpfe, den
    häßlichen Dünsten schwitzender Fette, überschäumender
    Milch?
Weil ich bauchige Mehltonnen hebe, Gewürzbüchschen öffne,
    Muskatnuß reibe,
Kräuter wiege, in gläserne Schale Saft der Zitrone presse,
    goldgelbes Dotter in blauem Becher zerquirle? …

To Serve

You who bind and dissolve, freeze and burn,
    weaken and reinforce Matter,
You who irritate acids, torment ore, hide secret mixtures in
    capsules, brew in tubes and crucibles
Even though neither the alkahest nor the white nor the red
    lion is what you are seething,
Initiate of an alchemy that appears strange and wonderful to me;
Master, you of the fire, which you tame in an iron cage, which,
    now crawling, cowers like a ready-to-jump, lying-in-wait
    beast of prey,
Which once sprung, smashed the bars, smote its furious claws
    around your limbs (oh, I am scared when I think of it!):
I want to lure another flame—gentle, tamed embers—which flatters
    and purrs and plays for me on the stove
    like a domesticated kitten;
Because I want to prepare colourful dishes, a little meal, which
    ought to delight you,
When you, weary and yet with a smile, turn to my darkening
    rooms.
Why do you all scold me?
Why do you all scorn me?
Because my world is shallow, hemmed in, only a few steps
    in a quadrat,
Full of inglorious petty things, insignificant chores,
Filled with the clatter of bowls, the bubbling of saucepans, the
    nasty steam of sweating grease, of foaming-over
    milk?
Because I lift bulbous flour drums, open little spice boxes,
    grate nutmeg,
Weigh herbs, press the juice of a lemon into a glass dish,
    whisk gold-yellow yolk in a blue goblet?...

Ja,
Wißt ihr denn, was die türkische kupferne Kaffemühle in
    Sarajewo sah
Und im böhmischen Eger mein Krug, leuchtend
    weißtupfig-rot wie Fliegenpilze des Waldes?
Wißt ihr,
Daß für mich große schwarzrauchende Schiffe alle Meere
    befahren, mit Fracht aller Küsten sich schleppen,
Daß, wenn die bleichen Körner durch meine Finger rieseln,
    stille Gesichter der Männer Ranguns mich schaun
Oder das dunklere Antlitz des Negers singt, der in den
    Reisfeldern Südcarolinas erntet?
Daß aus dem hölzernen Teekästchen unsichtbar eine Inderin
    steigt
Im Silberschmuck, in ocker- und terrakottfarb gewebtem
    Wallen und Wehen?
Aus Zwiebelschärfe hallen mir kräftige Stimmen bulgarischer
    Bauern wider,
Und ich frage zäh quellende Tropfen, ob nicht der Ölbaum
    meiner fremden, verlorenen Heimat sie schuf.

O sonnige Wiese, davon meine schmale, ängstliche Küche
    überfließt,
Mit dem Gürtel aus Natternkopf, Schafgarbe, Mäusegerste,
    Skabiosen,
Mit ruhig weidenden Scheckenkühn, dem rhythmischen
    Schlag ihrer Quastenschwänze,
O bräunlichgoldener Streif, den Mohnrot und Kornblumen-
    blau durchwirkt,
Den Mittagsstille umhaucht und der warme Duft künftigen
    Brotes! —
Da ich Krumen in die erhitzte brutzelnde Butter warf,
Schütterte noch aus geschwärzter Pfanne das Pochen von
    tausend Hämmern in Adern der Erde,

Well,
But, do you know what the Turkish copper coffee grinder saw
    in Sarajevo
And my jug in the Bohemian Eger,[3] radiant
    white-spotted-red, like fly-agarics of the forest?
Do you know
That for me big black-smoking ships travel all seas,
    hauling cargo from all coasts,
That, when the pale grains trickle through my fingers,
    calm faces of Rangoon men look at me,
Or the darker countenance of a Negro chants as he reaps
    in the paddy-fields of South Carolina?
That out of the small wooden tea-chest an Indian woman rises
    invisibly,
In silver jewellery, in ochre and terracotta-coloured
    woven flowing and fluttering?
Out of the sharpness of the onion strong voices of Bulgarian
    farmers resound towards me,
And I ask the slowly-oozing drips if it wasn't the olive tree
    of my lost alien homeland that had created them.

O sunny meadow, from which my narrow, anxious kitchen
    overflows
With the belt of blue borage, yarrow, wall barley,
    scabiosa,
With calmly grazing cows, the rhythmical
    beat of their tassels,
O brown-golden band, interwoven with red poppies and
    blue cornflowers,
Surrounded by the breath of midday stillness, and the warm scent of
    future bread! —
As I tossed crumbs into the heated, sizzling butter,
The knocking of a thousand hammers in the veins of the earth,
    still vibrated out of the blackened pan;

---

[3] Eger, now Cheb, was in the Sudetenland, but is now part of the Czech
Republic.

Zischte im Knistern noch immer empört gemartertes Eisen,
Das der Mutter geraubt, vergewaltigt in Öfen, zur Formung
    gezwungen ward.
Da von dampfender Suppe mein Löffel schmeckte, den
    kundige Hand geschnitzt,
Wuchs über niederes Dach wieder ein Lindenast,
Blühend, umtönt von Bienenchören.

Es komme mein Freund und esse.
Sieh, alles Wesen war mir zu Dienst, auf daß ich dem Einen
    diene.
Liebe deckte auch heut wie gestern den Tisch.
Nimm denn mit Liebe an, was die Schüssel trägt:
Möge es deinen Augen gefallen, sein Ruch dir angenehm
    sein, und was zum Munde eingeht, sei dir gesegnet!

Outraged tortured iron, robbed from the mother,
Violated in kilns, forced into forming,
      still hissed in the crackling.
When my spoon, carved by expert hands,
      tasted of steaming soup
A linden branch, in flower, grew again over low roof,
Enveloped by the sound of a choir of bees.

You may come, my friend, and eat.
See, all Being was at my service so that I could serve
      the One.
Love sets the table today as yesterday.
Accept then, with love, what the bowl yields:
May it please your eyes, its smell be agreeable to
      you, and what is received in the mouth be blessed for you!

Türme

Am Strande nördlichen Meeres,
Wo schwarzer grausamer Sturm Schwärme gell kreischender
    Möwen peitscht,
Wo an rissige Klippen geschleuderte Woge eisgrün klirrend
    zerbricht,
Zerschellt, zerspritzt,
Starrt der Turm.
Hart, finster, lastend, stumm in grauer Öde.
Erstorben.
Ohne Mund.
Kein Tor, keine Pforte: verschlossen.
Aus blicklosen Fenstern geistert in Nebeln düsterrot
    glimmendes Licht,
Kolkt ein Rabe krächzende Prophezeihungen,
Schwimmt Schneeeule lautlos, flockenrieselnd in das
    kristallen singende Schweigen der Nacht. —
Irgendwo fern klagt ein Schiff im Eise …

Irgendwo.

Irgendwo in Böhmen senkt eine Birke schmale blond
    umflossene Wangen rötlichen Trümmern zu.
Wehmütig, mit auf der Brust gefalteten Händen.
Doch um ihren Fuß spielen Glockenblumen,
Bunter Wachtelweizen belächelt das machtlose Burgverlies,
    und Gras trauert tändelnd auf der begrabenen Schwelle;
Feuerfalter gaukeln in Sonne über gestürzte Mauern, über
    erloschne Geschlechter hin.

Aus gierig glänzenden Augen der blauen Haie, die spähend,
    schnappend in Küstengewässern sich tummeln,
Blicken die Herrn der Feste, Seelen illyrischer Seeräuber her,

Towers

By the shores of the northern Sea,
Where cruel black storm lashes swarms of shrill
    shrieking gulls,
Where the wave, hurled at the fissured cliffs, jangling ice-green,
    shatters,
Smashes, sprays,
Stares the tower.
Harsh, grim, oppressive, mute in grey barrenness.
Petrified.
Without mouth.
No archway, no gate: bolted.
Out of unseeing windows emanates in mists a gloomy-red
    glimmering light,
A raven craws croaking prophesies,
A snowy-owl floats soundless, flake-fluttering into the
    crystal singing silence of the night. —
Somewhere far away a boat moans in the ice ...

Somewhere.

Somewhere in Bohemia, a birch dips sallow
    flowing slender cheeks towards reddish ruins.
Melancholic, with hands folded upon the breast.
But bell-flowers play around its foot,
Colourful cow-wheat smiles at the powerless dungeon,
    and grass mourns seductively on the buried threshold;
Butterflies[4] flutter in the sun over fallen walls, over
    extinct lineages.

Out of the greedily gleaming eyes of the blue sharks, which romp,
    scouting, snapping in the coastal waters,
Peer the masters of the feasts, the souls of Illyrian buccaneers,

---

[4] Kolmar has *Feuerfalter*, the small copper butterfly

Die einst den trotzig plumpen, vierschrötig niederen Bau
zum Hüter blitzender Beute setzten.
O schwarze Flaggen, Kaperfahrten, waffenschlagende
Plankenkämpfe mit den Venedigern!
Vorbei.
An den verfallenden Kammern
Läuten nicht trunken goldene Becher mehr, die blutfarbnen
Weines voll sind,
Dringt auch heut nicht Fischerkindergelärm, noch der
scharfe Ruch gebratenen Seefangs.
Jadeschimmernde Eidechsen huschen emsig schwänzelnd
umher, tuscheln in Eidechsmundart zusammen
Oder sitzen auf lichtumspülten, warmen Steinen geruhsam
sinnend.
In dunklen Mauern gebiert das Skorpionsweibchen lebende
Junge und stirbt; aber die Söhne erben der Väter Gift.

Auch dieser ist einsam.
Dem ein herrischer Mund zu sein gebot, die zeptertragende
Hand eines Königs im Osten.
Doch die Krone sprang von der Stirn, und die
myrrhenduftenden Prunkgewänder verdarben. —
Er aber steht und leidet.
Unsäglich leerer Himmel, der Vogelfittich und fruchtende
Wolke nicht kennt, gießt brennende Bläue endlos über
ihn aus;
Gluthitzen, Strahlenfluten rinnen von seinen bleichen
Quadern.
Die Zypresse floh. Zeder und Ölbaum sind fortgewandert,
und keine Rebe schmiegt liebende Arme um seinen
schlafenden Stein.
Kein Hirt treibt die Schafe, daß sie aus erdnahen Fugen ihm
staubige Gräser rupfen,
Und dem Zug beladner Kamele zeigt er niemals den Weg.

Zuweilen,
Wenn die Sichel der Nacht des Tages glühende Garben mäht,

Who once planted the defiantly plump, burly, low building
　　as the custodian of sparkling spoils.
O black flags, sea-faring, weapon-striking
　　plank fights with the Venetians!
Over.
By the dilapidating chambers
Intoxicated golden goblets full of blood coloured wine
　　no longer resound.
Also today neither the noise of fishermen's children nor the
　　sharp odour of fried sea-catch penetrates.
Jade-glimmering lizards, tail-wagging industriously, dart
　　around whispering together in lizard speak
Or perch on illuminated warm stones, musing
　　peacefully.
In dark walls the female scorpion gives birth to living
　　young and dies; but the sons inherit the fathers' poison.

This one is also solitary,
Which an imperious mouth, the sceptre-bearing
　　hand of a king in the east, commanded to be.
Yet the crown fell off the forehead, and the
　　myrrh-scented sumptuous garments were ruined. —
　But it stands and suffers.
　Unspeakably empty sky, which knows neither bird wing nor fruiting
　　cloud, pours burning blue endlessly
　　over it;
Sweltering heat, radiant beams run off its pale
　　ashlars.
The cypress fled. Cedar and olive tree have wandered away,
　　and no vine snuggles loving arms around its
　　sleeping stone.
No herdsman drives the sheep to pull up dusty grass for it
　　from the crannies near to the earth,
And it never points the way for the caravan of laden camels.

Occasionally,
When the sickle of the night reaps the glowing sheaves of the day,

Ein schmaler Mond wie Balsam ihm silbrige Kühle träuft,
Bebt aus seinem Wesen
Der scheue, leise, schnell ermattete Klang
Verschollener Harfe.

Vielleicht vergaß mich meine Seele im Traum,
Sank gen Morgen gebreitet, und ihres Wandelfluges
Harrte der weiße Turm: Durch seine heißen,
　　verwunschenen, lebenlosen Gemächer irrte sie,
Ihre Ahnen suchend,
Und rührte verschwebend Saiten an, die noch tönen …

And a slender moon, like balm, trickles silvery coolness for it,
Out of its essence trembles
The shy, soft, quickly faded sound
Of the harp lost without trace.

Perhaps my soul forgot me in the dream,
Subsided, spread out towards the morning,
And the white tower waited for her wandering flight:
    she erred through its hot enchanted lifeless chambers
Seeking for her ancestors
And hovering, touched strings that still resound ...

Die Tiere von Ninive

(Jona, Schlußwort.)

Die Nacht
Neigte goldblasse Schale, und Mondmilch troff
In das kupferne Becken
Auf dem Dache des weißen Hauses,
Und eine blaugraue Katze mit Agtsteinaugen
Schlich und hockte und trank.

In einer Nische bröckelnden Tempelgemäuers
Saß Racham der Geier regungslos mit gesunkenen Flügeln
Und schlief.
Fern
Hinter den Weingärten lag an wüstem Ort ein gestürzter,
    verendeter Esel.
In seinem gebrochenen Blick fraßen Würmer,
Und sein Geruch ward stinkend und befleckte die reine Luft
    und verhöhnte den leisen Tau, der ihn netzte.
Und er harrte spitzer, fallender Fittiche, des gelben, häßlich
    nackten Vogelgesichts, bohrender Krallen und des
    zerreißenden tilgenden Schnabels,
Auf daß bestattet werde, was Erde und Wind verpestet ...
Der Geier träumte.

Nah dem Tore der Stadt
Ruhte am Hügel, den gebogenen Stab zur Seite, ein junger
    Hirt.
Sein Knabenantlitz, erhoben wie leerer empfangender
    Becher, füllte sich schimmernd mit dem rieselnden
    Licht der Gestirne,
Quoll über,
Und ihr schwebend sirrendes, singendes Kreisen in
    unendlichen Räumen rührte sein Ohr.
Rings zerging das weiche Vließ seiner Lämmer in dunstig
    dünnes Gewölk.

The Animals of Nineveh

(Jonah, epilogue.)

The night
Inclined the pale gold bowl, and moon-milk dripped
Into the copper basin
Upon the roof of the white house,
And a blue-grey cat with agate stone eyes
Crept and crouched and drank.

In a niche of the crumbling temple walls
Sat Racham the vulture motionless with sunken wings
And slept.
Far away
Behind the vineyards, in a desolate place, lay a fallen
    donkey that had perished.
Worms fed in its broken gaze,
And its smell became foetid and sullied the pure air
    and mocked the soft dew which moistened it.
And it waited for the sharp, dropping wings, the yellow,
    ugly naked bird-face, for the drilling claws and the
    tearing, erasing beak,
So that what pollutes earth and wind would be buried ...
The vulture dreamed.

Near the city gate
A young shepherd rested by the hill, the bent staff
    to one side.
His boyish countenance, raised like an empty receiving
    cup filled itself shimmering with the fluttering
    light of the stars,
Welled over,
And their floating, susurrating orbit chanting in
    infinite spheres, touched his ears.
Around him the soft fleece of his lambs melted into misty
    thin clouds.

Ein Kind,
Kleiner abgezehrter, schmutziger Leib,
Bedeckt mit Fetzen, bedeckt mit Schwären,
Über die Schwelle der Grabkammer hingeworfen,
Streckte sich, schlief.
Es kannte nicht Vater noch Mutter, und nur ein Hund,
Einer der Ausgestoßenen, Verachtetsten,
Gleich arm, gleich krank, geplagt und zerschrunden,
Kratzte sich, duckte den Kopf und leckte liebreich die
    Wange unter den strähnig schwarzen verfilzten
    Haaren. —
Und das Kind ballte die Faust und schlug ihn im Traum.

Und ein Sturm flog auf mit mächtigem Braus,
Ein großer Sturm fuhr von Osten auf und kam und fegte
    die Weide, entsetzte die Herden und wirbelte totes
    Geäst
Und griff wie mit Nägeln in des Propheten Bart, zerrte und
    zauste.

Doch Jona ging,
Und die Last über Ninive, die er geschaut, hing über seinem
    Scheitel.
Er aber wandelte in schwerem Sinnen. —

Von der starken Säule des Königsschlosses schmetterte ein
    bemalter Stein,
Und es heulte im Sturm und es schrie im Sturme und eine
    Stimme rief:
»Um dieser willen!
Um dieser Tiere, reiner und unreiner, willen!«
Und der Gesandte des Herrn schrak und sah; aber nur
    Finsternis war, und er hörte nichts als ein unablässiges
    Wehen und Sausen,
Das seinen Mantel faßte und zog und schüttelte wie eines
    Bittenden Hand das Kleid des unbarmherzig
    Enteilenden.

A child,
Small, emaciated, dirty body,
Covered with rags, covered with sores,
Flung across the threshold of the burial chamber,
Stretched himself, slept.
He did not know father or mother, and only a dog,
One of the outcasts, the most despised,
Equally poor, equally sick, tormented and torn,
Scratched itself, cowered the head and lovingly licked
     the cheek under the straggly black matted
     hair. —
And the child clenched the fist and beat it in the dream.

And a storm arose with a mighty roar,
A great storm drove in from the east and came and swept
     the meadow, terrified the herds and whirled dead
     branches
And, as if with nails, seized the prophet's beard, tugged and
     tousled.

But Jonah went,
And the burden upon Nineveh, which he had beheld, hung over his
     head
He, however, walked in deep musing. —

A painted stone smashed from the strong column
     of the king's palace,
And there was a wailing in the storm and a yelling in the storm and a
     voice called;
"For the sake of those!
For the sake of those animals, clean and unclean!"
And the envoy of the Lord took fright and saw; but there was only
     darkness, and he heard nothing but an incessant
     blowing and roaring,
Which seized his cloak and tugged and shook it, like a
     beggar's hand seizes at the garment of the merciless one who
     hastens away.

Er aber kehrte sich nicht; er schritt
Und raffte und hielt den Mantel.

But he didn't care; he strode
And gathered and held onto the cloak.

Der Engel im Walde

Gib mir deine Hand, die liebe Hand, und komm mit mir;
Denn wir wollen hinweggehen von den Menschen.
Sie sind klein und böse, und ihre kleine Bosheit haßt und
   peinigt uns.
Ihre hämischen Augen schleichen um unser Gesicht, und ihr
   gieriges Ohr betastet das Wort unseres Mundes.
Sie sammeln Bilsenkraut ...
So laß uns fliehn
Zu den sinnenden Feldern, die freundlich mit Blumen und
   Gras unsere wandernden Füße trösten,
An den Strom, der auf seinem Rücken geduldig wuchtende
   Bürden, schwere, güterstrotzende Schiffe, trägt,
Zu den Tieren des Waldes, die nicht übelreden.
Komm.
Herbstnebel schleiert und feuchtet das Moos mit dumpf
   smaragdenem Leuchten.
Buchenlaub rollt, Reichtum goldbronzener Münzen.
Vor unseren Schritten springt, rote zitternde Flamme, das
   Eichhorn auf.
Schwarze gewundene Erlen züngeln am Pfuhl empor in
   kupfriges Abendglasten.

Komm.
Denn die Sonne ist nieder in ihre Höhle gekrochen und ihr
   warmer rötlicher Atem verschwebt.
Nun tut ein Gewölb sich auf.
Unter seinem graublauen Bogen zwischen bekrönten Säulen
   der Bäume wird der Engel stehn,
Hoch und schmal, ohne Schwingen.
Sein Antlitz ist Leid.
Und sein Gewand hat die Bleiche eisig blinkender Sterne in
   Winternächten.
Der Seiende,

The Angel in the Forest

Give me your hand, the dear hand, and come with me;
Because we want to walk away from the people.
They are small and wicked, and their small wickedness detests and
    torments us,
Their spiteful eyes creep around our face, and their
    greedy ear gropes the word of our mouth.
They gather henbane ...
So let us flee
To the musing fields, which congenially console our roaming feet
    with flowers and grass,
To the river, patiently bearing on its back heaving burdens,
    heavy freight-bursting ships,
To the animals of the forest who don't speak evil.
Come.
Autumn mist veils and dampens the moss with a dull
    emerald glow.
Beech leaves roll, an abundance of gold-bronze coins.
In front of our steps leaps a red quivering flame,
    the squirrel.
By the mire, black winding alders lick upwards into
    copper evening splendour.

Come.
Because the sun has crept down into its hollow, and its
    warm reddish breath has floated away.
Now a vault opens up.
Under its grey-blue arc, between crowned columns
    of trees, the angel will stand,
Tall and slender without wings.
His countenance is sorrow.
And his robe has the pallor of icy gleaming stars in
    winter nights.
The Being,

Der nicht sagt, nicht soll, der nur *ist*,
Der keinen Fluch weiß noch Segen bringt und nicht in Städte
    hinwallt zu dem, was stirbt:
Er schaut uns nicht
In seinem silbernen Schweigen.
Wir aber schauen ihn,
Weil wir zu zweit und verlassen sind.

Vielleicht
Weht ein braunes, verwelktes Blatt an seine Schulter, entgleitet;
Das wollen wir aufheben und verwahren, ehe wir weiterziehn.

Komm, mein Freund, mit mir, komm.
Die Treppe in meines Vaters Hause ist dunkel und krumm
    und eng, und die Stufen sind abgetreten;
Aber jetzt ist es das Haus der Waise und fremde Leute wohnen
    darin.
Nimm mich fort.
Schwer fügt der alte rostige Schlüssel im Tor sich meinen
    schwachen Händen.
Nun knarrt es zu.
Nun sieh mich an in der Finsternis, du, von heut meine Heimat.
Denn deine Arme sollen mir bergende Mauern baun,
Und dein Herz wird mir Kammer sein und dein Auge mein
    Fenster, durch das der Morgen scheint.
Und es türmt sich die Stirn, da du schreitest.
Du bist mein Haus an allen Straßen der Welt, in jeder Senke,
    auf jedem Hügel.
Du Dach, du wirst ermattet mit mir unter glühendem Mittag
    lechzen, mit mir erschauern, wenn Schneesturm peitscht.
Wir werden dürsten und hungern, zusammen erdulden,
Zusammen einst an staubigem Wegesrande sinken und
    weinen …

Who does not say, no should, who just *is*,
Who knows no curse, brings no blessings and does not surge into cities,
    towards that which dies:
He does not behold us
In his silver silence.
But we behold him,
Because we are two and forsaken.

Perhaps
A brown faded leaf blows against his shoulder, slides down;
We want to pick this up and keep it, before we move on.

Come with me, my friend, come.
The stairs in my father's house are dark and crooked
    and narrow, and the steps are worn;
But now it is the house of the orphan and strangers live
    in it.
Take me away.
The old rusty key in the gate hardly obeys my
    feeble hands.
Now it creaks shut.
Now look at me in the darkness, you, from today my home.
Because your arms shall build me sheltering walls,
And your heart will be my chamber and your eye my
    window through which the morning shines.
And the forehead towers up as you stride.
You are my house on all the streets of the world, in every valley,
    on every hill.
You roof, you will thirst wearily with me under sweltering midday,
    shiver with me when snow storm whips.
We will thirst and hunger, suffer together,
Together one day sink down by the dusty wayside verge and
    weep...

Aus dem Dunkel

Aus dem Dunkel komme ich, eine Frau.
Ich trage ein Kind und weiß nicht mehr, wessen;
Einmal hab' ich's gewußt.
Aber nun ist kein Mann mehr für mich ...
Alle sind hinter mir eingesunken wie Rinnsal,
Das die Erde trank.
Ich gehe weiter und weiter.
Denn ich will vor Tag ins Gebirge, und die Gestirne
    schwinden schon.

Aus dem Dunkel komme ich.
Durch finstere Gassen schritt ich einsam,
Da jäh vorstürzendes Licht mit Krallen die sanfte Schwärze
    zerriß,
Der Pardel die Hirschkuh,
Und weit aufgestoßene Tür häßliches Kreischen, wüstes
    Gejohle, tierisches Brüllen spie.
Trunkene wälzten sich ...
Ich schüttelte das am Wege vom Saum meines Kleides.

Und ich wanderte über den verödeten Markt.
Blätter schwammen in Lachen, die den Mond spiegelten.
Magere, gierige Hunde berochen Abfälle auf den Steinen.
Früchte faulten zertreten,
Und ein Greis in Lumpen quälte noch immer sein armes
    Saitenspiel
Und sang mit dünner, mißtönig klagender Stimme
Ungehört.
Und diese Früchte waren einst in Sonne und Tau gereift,
Träumend noch vom Duft und Glück der liebenden Blüte,
Doch der wimmernde Bettler
Vergaß das längst und kannte nichts anderes mehr als Hunger
    und Durst.

Out of the Darkness

Out of the darkness I come, a woman.
I carry a child and know no more, whose;
Once I knew it.
But now no man is for me anymore....
All behind me have disappeared like a rivulet,
Which the earth drank.
I go on and on.
Because I want to be in the mountains before day-break and the stars
    are already fading.

Out of the darkness I come.
I strode lonely through dark alley-ways,
When light suddenly leapt out, tore apart the gentle blackness
    with claws,
The leopard, the hind,
And the door, pushed wide open, spewed out ugly screeching,
    wild shouting, animalistic roars.
Drunkards writhed ....
Along the way I shook that off the hem of my dress.

And I wandered across the deserted market.
Leaves swam in pools reflecting the moon.
Mangy, greedy dogs sniffed litter on the stones.
Trampled fruits putrefied,
And an old man in rags still tortured his poor
    stringed instrument
And with thin, tunelessly lamenting voice sang
Unheard.
And these fruits once ripened in sun and dew,
Still dreaming of the scent and happiness of the loving blossom,
But the whimpering beggar
Had long since forgotten this and no longer knew anything but hunger
    and thirst.

Vor dem Schlosse des Mächtigen stand ich still,
Und da ich die unterste Stufe trat,
Zerbarst der fleischrote Porphyr knackend an meiner Sohle. —
Ich wendete mich
Und schaute empor zu dem kahlen Fenster, der späten Kerze
    des Denkenden,
Der sann und sann und nie seiner Frage Erlösung fand,
Und zu dem verhüllten Lämpchen des Kranken, der doch
    nicht lernte,
Wie er sterben sollte.
Unter dem Brückenbogen
Zankten zwei scheußliche Gerippe sich um Gold.
Ich hob meine Armut als grauen Schild vor mein Antlitz
Und zog ungefährdet vorbei.

Im Fernen redet der Fluß mit seinen Ufern.

Nun strauchl' ich den steinigen, widerstrebenden Pfad hinan.
Felsgeröll, Stachelsträucher verwunden die blinden, tastenden
    Hände:
Eine Höhle wartet,
Die im tiefsten Geklüft den erzgrünen Raben herbergt, der
    keinen Namen hat.
Da werde ich eingehn,
Unter dem Schutz der großen schattenden Schwinge mich
    niederkauern und ruhn,
Verdämmernd dem stummen wachsenden Wort meines
    Kindes lauschen
Und schlafen, die Stirn gen Osten geneigt,
Bis Sonnenaufgang.

I stood still in front of the castle of the Powerful,
And as I trod the lowest step,
The flesh-red Porphyry burst apart cracking at my sole. —
I turned
And looked up at the barren window, at the late candle
     of the Thinker,
Who mused and mused and never found his question's release,
And to the little veiled lamp of the sick-one who just
     did not learn
How he should die.
Under the arch of the bridge
Two hideous skeletons squabbled over gold.
I lifted my poverty like a grey shield in front of my countenance
And passed by unharmed.

Far off the river talks with its banks.

Now I stumble up the stony, recalcitrant path.
Loose rocks, thorny shrubs wound the blind, feeling
     hands:
A cavern is waiting,
Which in the deepest chasms shelters the mineral-green Raven that
     has no name.
There I will enter,
Huddle myself down and rest under the protection of the big
     shadow-giving wing.
Drowsily listening to the silent growing word
     of my child
And sleep, the forehead bowed to the East,
Until sunrise.

Asien

Mutter,
Die du mir warst, eh' mich die meine wiegte,
Ich kehre heim.
Laß mich hintreten vor dich.
Laß mich still dir zu Füßen sitzen, dich anschaun, dich
    lernen:
Den stolzen verhüllten Wuchs, mächtig ragend von
    mythischen Throne,
Der da auf Säulen weißer steinerner Elefantenfüße ruht,
Zu dessen Armlehne jadezüngiger bronzener Drache wurde,
Dein ernstes sonnengelbliches Antlitz, das blauschwarzes
    Haar seiden umspinnt,
Die Stirn, Hegemauer großer Gedanken,
Und deine Augen, jetzt finster glänzender Obsidian,
Dann wieder samten und tief, dunkle Urwaldsblumen.
Laß an deine Gewänder mich rühren, die Ruch von Ambra
    und Myrrhe, von Sandel und Zimmet wehn,
Die flammenden, indischem Webstuhl entlodert,
Und jene maisblassen, drauf ein Chinesenmädchen braunen
    Zweig, Mandelblüte und kleine rostfarbne Falter
    gestickt hat.
Weise mir deine Kronen: die südliche,
Grüngoldnes Palmenlaub, perlenbetaut, von Turmalin und
    Smaragd, Hyazinth und Saphir durchblüht,
Und die nördliche, funkelnd von Eiskristall, mit den
    Aquamarintropfen der sibirischen Meere.
Meinen Scheitel streife die Hand, deren Fläche noch Duft
    und Schmelz persischer Früchte hält,
Und mein Ohr umspiele Schalmeiensingen, wie es David der
    Hirt einst in den Gefilden Beth-Lechems übte.

Asia

Mother,
You who were for me, before mine cradled me,
I return home.
Let me step before you.
Let me sit still by your feet, look at you,
    study you:
The proud veiled stature, powerfully rising from a
    mythical throne
That rests there on columns of white stone elephant feet,
A jade-tongued bronze dragon became its arm rest,
Your solemn sun-yellow countenance, which blue-black
    hair silkily encompasses,
The brow, protective wall of great thoughts,
And your eyes, now sinister shining obsidian,
Then velvet and deep, dark primeval forest flowers.
Let me touch your robes, which waft the scent of amber
    and myrrh, of sandalwood and cinnamon,
The fiery ones, flared up out of Indian looms,
And those corn-pale ones, onto which a Chinese girl has embroidered
    a brown branch, an almond blossom and small
    rust-coloured butterflies.
Show me your crowns: the southern one,
Green-golden palm leaves, dewy-pearled, entwined with tourmaline and
    emeralds, hyacinth and sapphire,
And the northern one, sparkling with ice crystal, with the
    aquamarine drops of Siberian seas.
Let the crown of my head be kissed by the hand whose palm still holds
    the scent and melting of Persian fruits,
And let my ear be charmed by the singing of shawms, as David the
    herdsman once practised it in the realms of Beth-Lechem.[5]

---

[5] The house of bread.

Du Sinnende, Glühende, du, die adligste, reichste und reifste
    der Schwestern:
Du anders als jene seltsame dunkelhäutige,
Die bald mit dem Skarabäusring ihres Fingers Einlaß
    fordernd an riesig steinerne Wohnungen toter Könige
    pocht,
Bald wieder, Straußenfeder und Muschel im wolligen Haar,
    Pygmäen durch Wälder treibt
Oder in Wüstenleere falbmähnige Löwen weidet.
Anders du als die kindlich jüngste, die mit des Känguruhs
    drolligen Sprüngen hüpft
Und Händevoll grasgrüner Sittiche über den Buschstrand
    des Murray ausstreut.

Anders ...

Du hast noch die stumme unendliche Geduld,
Das Wissen vom Nicht-Tun, gewaltiger Ruhe, die in sich
    versunken träumt,
Dein ist die Schau,
Der rätselnde Aufblick in blaue Nacht zu leuchtend
    wandelnden Welten.
Du bist, ob du nicht wirkst.
Und sprichst mit dem leichten Heben schmaler gülden
    bestäubter Hand, mit sanfter Wendung schlangen-
    biegsamen Halses
Und hörst den Ruf des Saxaulhähers,
Der deiner Einöde Kysyl-kum roten Sand durchwirbelt und
    des Wasserquells nicht bedarf,
Und weißt das Märchen des Rock, dessen unermeßlicher Flug
    dein Haupt überschattet.
Um dich ist Ferne.
Du sitzest,
Zaubernde hinter gläserner Wand,
Geschieden, doch nah, sichtbar, unfaßlich.
Draußen ziehn sie dahin,

You contemplative one, you glowing one, you, the noblest, richest
    and maturest of the sisters:
You, different from the strange, dark-skinned one,
Who sometimes, with a scarab ring on her finger, pounds at
    the colossal stone dwellings of the dead kings, demanding
    admission,
Other times, ostrich feather and shell in woolly hair, drives
    pygmies through forests
Or grazes dusky maned lions in desolate wilderness.
You, different from the childish youngest, who hops with
    the droll bounds of the kangaroo
And scatters handfuls of grass-green parakeets over
    The Murray's shrubby shore.

Different...

You still have the infinite silent patience,
The knowledge of the not-doing, of immense calm, which,
    absorbed in itself, dreams,
Yours is the vision,
The enigmatic gaze into the blue night towards the radiant
    ever changing worlds.
You are, though you do nothing.
And you speak with the slight lift of a slender hand
    pollinated with gold, with the gentle turn of the lithesome
    snaking neck
And you hear the cry of the panders ground-jay,
Who whirls through the red sand of your Kysyl-kum desert,
    and has no need of the water source,
And you know the fairy-tale of the Roc whose immeasurable flight
    casts a shadow over your head.
Around you is distance.
You sit,
Sorceress behind a glass wall,
Separated, but near, visible, incomprehensible.
Outside they pass by,

Träger, die dir aus bauchigen Schiffen Ballen und Kisten und
    Körbe höhlen, Geschenke:
Jahrmarktsglück, Flitterspiel, Klapperlärmen, billig
    armseligen Prunk …
Draußen bettelt und nimmt und rafft dein eigenes Abbild,
    Schemen,
Der Seiden, lieblich wie Krokus und Orchidee, mit häßlich
    schwarzem englischen Tuch vertauschte
Und deines Sehers Sprüche, die blühenden, vieltausend-
    jährig verzweigten Äste, um graue Büschel dürr und
    geschwätzig knisternder Blätter gab.
Sie ahmt, die gespenstische Magd, dir Herrscherin nach,
    heuchelt deine Gebärde, dein Wort, stiehlt deinen
    Namen,
Wenn du hinabgetaucht zum tiefen Innen unseres Sterns,
    dem Bade schäumenden Feuers …

Brenne …
Birg voll Scham, was die Törichte blößt, deiner Mitte
    Geheimnis, das Flammensamen empfing,
Und die Geborenen, Geierdämonen, laß ewiglich kreisen
    über den Totentürmen,
Türmen des Schweigens …

Porters, who hollow out bales and crates and baskets, gifts for you
  from out of bulbous ships:
Luck of the fair, trinkets, noisy clatter-rattles, cheap pitiful
  splendour...
Outside, your own image begs and takes and grabs,
  a spectre
That exchanged silks, delightful like crocus and orchid, for ugly
  black English fabric
And squandered the aphorisms of your prophet, the blossoming, many
  thousand year old branched boughs, for grey bundles of barren
  and prattling, crackling leaves.
She, the ghostly maid, mimics you, the Queen, feigns
  your gesture, your word, steals your
  name,
When you have dived down to the deep inside of our star,
  to the pool of foaming fire...

Burn ...
Hide full of shame what the foolish one uncovers, the secret of your
  core, which received the fiery seeds,
And the ones who were born, vulture demons, let them circle eternally
  over the towers of the dead,
The towers of silence...

Barsoi

Dein war das Dunkel, die Höhle des Mutterleibes.
Dein war der Grund, Erde, die Tiere trägt.
Blind krochst du, suchend und saugend, unter den Zitzen der
    Hündin umher
Und nährtest dich, wuchsest und wurdest sehend
Und spieltest zwischen Geschwistern ...
Weißt du noch?
Nein, du weißt nichts mehr.
Kaum kennst du dies Fell, das dir wallt, weißflockig
    schäumende See um isabellfarbne Inseln.

Liebliche du, Anmutige, mit dem schmalen, gestreckten
    Haupt, den sanften, braunen, glänzenden Mandelaugen,
Du träumst
Nördliche blasse Birken im Moor, dem schwärzlich
    brandiges Ungeheuer, der schaufelhörnige Elch, entloht;
Dein Blut
Hetzt noch den grauen Wolf durch Tannenfinsternis
    russischer Wälder,
Spürt noch weidende Renntierherden über Moos und Flechte
    der Tundra,
Hört noch angstvolles Jammern, des Eishasen Klageschrei
Vor dem Jäger ...

Tags
Ruhest du still auf der Decke und hebst mir dein
    Frauenantlitz mit jener Milde der Hindin, des Einhorns
    entgegen,
Oder du läufst gesenkten Kopfes, schnupperst und scharrst
    an Komposthaufen, Büschen und Beeten, wie Hunde tun.

In Herbstnächten,
Da starke, kältere Sterne flimmern,

Borzoi

Yours was the darkness, the cavern of the mother-body.
Yours was the ground, the earth that carries animals.
You crawled around blind, seeking and sucking under the teats
    of the bitch
And nourished yourself, grew and became seeing
And played between brothers and sisters ...
Do you still remember?
No you don't remember anything anymore.
You hardly know this coat that flows upon you, white-fluffy
    foaming sea, around isabel-coloured islands.

You lovely one, graceful one, with the slender stretched
    head, the gentle, brown gleaming almond eyes,
You dream
Northern pale birches on the moor, from which the blackish
    burnt monster, the shovel-horned elk, blazes forth;
Your blood
Still hounding the grey wolf through pine darkness
    of Russian forests,
Still tracking grazing reindeer-herds across moss and lichen
    of the tundra,
Still hearing the fearful wailing, the lamenting cry of the snow hare
Before the huntsman ...

By day
You rest silently on the rug and, with the gentleness
    of the hind, the unicorn, lift your woman's face
    towards me,
Or you run head down, like dogs do, sniffing and scratching
    at the compost mounds, bushes and borders.

In autumn nights,
When stronger, colder stars flicker,

Hin und wieder vom Baume fallender Tropfen tönt,
Da gilbendes Gras Frische und Feuchte atmet,
Zieh' ich den Mantel um meine Schultern, öffne die eiserne
Tür
Des Gartens;
Du jagst in riesigen Sätzen.
Du fliegst, du stiebst
Schneesturmgleich über den Teppich welker, triefender
Blätter;
Silbern wehende Flamme, lodert dein mähniger Schweif dir
nach.
Und ich gehe und rufe dich mit dumpferer Stimme, und du
harrst, hoch und leicht, hauchfahl, ein Schemen an
Wegeswende.
Du stehst und starrst.
Was erblickst du?
Glosten am Faulbaum, in Geißblattsträuchern gelbe Augen
auf, Katzenaugen, die du hassest?
Tritt ein Gespenst, die Flatterhände voll blutiger Gekröse,
dich an — und deine lange Nase wittert die Beute?
Bist du nur Wohnung fremder, unfaßlicher Seele, die
zuzeiten das Tierhaus läßt als wesenlose durchsichtige
Hülle?
Sie irrt
Über Rasen, zwischen den bronzenen Chrysanthemen, und
du wartest auf Wiederkehr.
Naht sie?
Meine Finger berühren die Kühle und Glätte der Echsen-
stirn … ein Halsband klimpert.
Folgsam trabt neben mir die bleiche und stumme Gefährtin
heim.

Occasional drip resounds falling off the tree,
When yellowing grass breathes freshness and moistness,
I pull the coat around my shoulders, open the iron
    door
Of the garden;
You chase in colossal bounds.
You fly, you spatter
Like a snowstorm over the carpet of withered dripping
    leaves;
Silver fluttering flame, your mane-like tail flares after
    you.
And I go and call you with more muffled voice, and you
    alert, tall and light, ghost-pale, a silhouette by
    the turn of the road.
You stand and stare.
What do you descry?
Did yellow eyes glow in the honeysuckle bushes by the alder-buckthorn,
    cats eyes which you hate?
Is a ghost stepping towards you, fluttering hands full of bloody offal —
    and your long nose sniffs the prey?
Are you just home to an alien, incomprehensible soul, which
    at times leaves the animal house as a beingless transparent
    shell?
She roams
Over the lawns, between the bronze chrysanthemums, and
    you wait for the return.
Is she approaching?
My fingers touch the coolness and smoothness of the lizard-
    forehead ... a collar tinkles.
Obedient beside me, the pale and silent companion trots
    homeward.

Die alte Frau

Heut bin ich krank, nur heute, und morgen bin ich gesund.
Heut bin ich arm, nur heute, und morgen bin ich reich.
Einst aber werde ich immer so sitzen,
In dunkles Schultertuch frierend verkrochen, mit
    hüstelnder, rasselnder Kehle,
Mühsam hinschlurfen und an den Kachelofen knöchrige
    Hände tun.
Dann werde ich alt sein.

Meiner Haare finstere Amselschwingen sind grau,
Meine Lippen bestaubte, verdorrte Blüten,
Und nichts weiß mein Leib mehr vom Fallen und Steigen der
    roten springenden Brunnen des Blutes.
Ich starb vielleicht
Lange schon vor meinem Tode.

Und doch war ich jung.
War lieb und recht einem Manne wie das braune nährende
    Brot seiner hungrigen Hand,
War süß wie ein Labetrunk seinem dürstenden Munde.
Ich lächelte
Und meiner Arme weiche, schwellende Nattern lockten
    umschlingend in Zauberwald.
Aus meiner Schulter sproßte rauchblauer Flügel,
Und ich lag an der breiteren buschigen Brust,
Abwärts rauschend, ein weißes Wasser, vom Herzen des
    Tannenfelsens.

Aber es kam der Tag und die Stunde kam,
Da das bittere Korn in Reife stand, da ich ernten mußte.
Und die Sichel schnitt meine Seele.
»Geh',« sprach ich, »Lieber, geh'.
Siehe, mein Haar weht Altweiberfäden,

The Old Woman

Today I am ill, only today, and tomorrow I am healthy.
Today I am poor, only today, and tomorrow I am rich.
But one day I will always sit like this,
Chilled, huddled up in a dark stole, with
	slightly coughing, rattling throat,
Shuffling along laboriously and putting bony hands on
	the tiled stove.
Then I will be old.

The dark blackbird wings of my hair are grey,
My lips dusty, dried up blossoms,
And my body no longer knows anything of the falling and rising of the
	red leaping fountains of the blood.
Maybe I died
Already long before my death.

And yet I was young.
Was just right for a man, like the brown nourishing
	bread for his hungry hand,
Was sweet like a refreshing draught for his thirsty mouth.
I smiled,
And the soft swelling serpents of my arms beckoned,
	entwining in an enchanted wood.
From my shoulder sprouted a smoke blue wing,
And I lay beside the broader bushy chest,
A white water rushing downwards from the heart of the
	pine rock.

But the day came and the hour came,
When the bitter seed stood ripened, when I had to reap.
And the sickle sliced my soul.
"Go", I said, "Beloved, go!
Look, my hair wafts gossamer threads,

Abendnebel näßt schon die Wange,
Und meine Blume schauert welkend in Frösten.
Furchen durchziehn mein Gesicht,
Schwarze Gräben die herbstliche Weide.
Geh'; denn ich liebe dich sehr.«

Still nahm ich die goldene Krone vom Haupt und verhüllte
　　mein Antlitz.
Er ging,
Und seine heimatlosen Schritte trugen wohl anderem
　　Rastort ihn zu unter helleren Augensternen.

Meine Augen sind trüb geworden und bringen Garn und
　　Nadelöhr kaum noch zusammen.
Meine Augen tränen müde unter den faltig schweren,
　　rotumränderten Lidern.
Selten
Dämmert wieder aus mattem Blick der schwache,
　　fernvergangene Schein
Eines Sommertages,
Da mein leichtes, rieselndes Kleid durch Schaumkraut-
　　wiesen floß
Und meine Sehnsucht Lerchenjubel in den offenen Himmel
　　warf.

Evening mist already moistens the cheek,
And my flower shudders withering in frosts.
Furrows cut through my face,
Black trenches through the autumnal meadow.
Go; because I love you so."

Silently I took the golden crown from the head and veiled
    my countenance.
He went,
And perhaps his homeless steps carried him to another
    resting place under brighter starry eyes.

My eyes have become dull and hardly bring needle eye and
    thread together.
My eyes water wearily under the wrinkled-heavy,
    red-rimmed eye-lids.
Occasionally
The faint long gone glow of a summer's day
    dawns from the dull eyes again,
One summer's day,
When my light fluttering dress flowed through the
    cuckoo-flower meadows
And my yearning threw lark's jubilation into the
    open sky.

Garten im Sommer

Gar nichts anderes war's; kein Vogel, kein Falter flog.
Nur ein gilbendes Blatt zitterte in den umsponnenen Weiher,
    ich sah es.
Komm.
Ach, dies tauig hauchende Gras, wie es zärtlich meine
    fiebrigen Zehen kühlt!
Bück' dich ein wenig:
Haselnüsse, die wohl der große plündernde Buntspecht
    hierher verstreut hat.
Aber noch sind sie nicht reif.
Nein, ich bin nicht genäschig noch hungrig.
Später werden wir unter die Obstbäume gehn und auf dem
    Rasen schöne rotflammige Äpfel suchen
Oder die runden, saftigen goldgrünen Pflaumen schütteln.
    Ja, willst du?
Weißt du noch: all die Pfauenaugen, so viele, die an den
    abgefallnen, verrotteten Früchten sogen und taumelten?
Und auch ein Trauermantel wehte, finsterer Sammet, gülden
    umsäumt, blau beperlt …
O die Rose! Sie duftet … Gestern noch wollte sie Knospe
    bleiben;
Nun schloß Nacht sie auf, daß sie blühe, die scheue, errötende,
    und sie scheint glücklich …
Du Geliebter, im Traum der Hummeln und Bienen muß
    solch unberührt schwebender alabasterner Becher glühn.
Du fragst mich, ob Bienen und Hummeln träumen?
Sicher träumen sie, wenn sie in jener rahmweißen
    Schwertel schlummern, kindlich von süßer, schaumiger
    Bienenmilch.
Aber Steinhummeln sind die schönsten, summend in warmen
    schwarz und fuchsigen Pelzen …
Was blickst du auf einmal seltsam mich an und lächelst?
War ich bleich schimmernd in Mitternächten dir
    berauschender Kelch?

Garden in Summer

It was nothing else; no bird, no butterfly flew.
Only a yellowing leaf quivered into the encompassed pond
    I saw it.
Come.
Oh, this dewy soft-breathing grass, how tenderly it cools
    my feverish toes!
Bend a little:
Hazelnuts: the large pillaging spotted woodpecker may
    have scattered them here.
But they are not yet ripe.
No, I am neither peckish nor hungry.
Later we will go beneath the fruit trees and search on the
    lawn for beautiful red-flaming apples,
Or shake the round, juicy gold-green plums.
    Yes, will you?
Do you still remember: all those Peacock butterflies, so many, that
    sucked on the fallen rotted fruits and swayed?
And also a Mourning Cloak fluttered, dark velvet, golden-
    hemmed, pearled blue ...
O the rose! She perfumes ... Yesterday she still wanted to stay
    in bud;
Now night unlocked her, so she could flower, the shy, blushing one,
    and she seems happy ...
You beloved one, in the dream of the bumble-bees and bees
    such untouched-floating alabaster cup must glow.
You ask me if bees and bumble-bees dream?
Sure they dream of sweet foaming bees-milk,
    when they slumber childlike in this
    cream-white lily.
But stone bumble-bees are the most beautiful, buzzing in warm
    black and gingery furs ...
Why do you suddenly look at me strangely and smile?
Was I your intoxicating chalice, shimmering
    pale in midnights?

Dir Milch, dir Wein, goldbrauner Malaga, rubinenes
    Kirschenwasser?
Schweig'. Ich lege die atmende Hand auf deine Lippen …

Morgenwind. Leise schauernde Halme. Feuchte.
Und ein winziger reglos hockender Frosch, der aus grüner
    Bronze geformt ist.
Und eine Seejungfer, stahlblau mit gläsernen Flügeln,
Sirrt dahin. Mich fröstelt …
Weiden wie badende Fraun neigen die Stirnen, fahlblond
    rieselndes Haar dem Teich.

Sprich, bedeutet ein Schneckenhorn Gutes dem, der es
    aufhebt?
Wenn du zweifelst, schenk' ich's der Flut.
Wie sie sich kräuselt, sich bauscht … seiden … und blinkt
    doch Kälte.
Hier auf dem einzig offnen, besonnten Fleckchen im
    Röhricht, Lieber, lass' noch ein wenig uns sitzen
Und hinüberschaun nach den Fenstern, unseren Fenstern,
    die Waldrebe und dumpferer Efeu umkriechen.
Wie mir dies kleine umschattete, weltversunkene Schloß
    gefällt!
Auch das Mauergeschnörkel, auch die geschwärzte
    Vergoldung, die bröckelnden Putten, die müden
    Blumengewinde,
Auch das Moos, das an den zersprungenen griechischen
    Vasen hängt.
Auch am Tor die mächtige Linde und ihre Ringeltaube, die
    wieder mit dunkelndem Rucksen ruft.
Und das kunstvoll geschmiedete Gitter …

Gehst du jetzt … soll ich schon folgen? Führ' mich; ich
    friere … ich fürchte …
Bis zu den Mummeln, dem gelben Leuchten, möchte ich
    schwimmen.

Your milk, your wine, gold-brown Malaga,
    ruby kirsch?
Be quiet. I lay the breathing hand on your lips ...

Morning wind. Faint trembling blades of grass. Moisture.
And a tiny motionlessly squatting frog, formed out
    of green bronze.
And a damsel fly, steel blue with glassy wings,
Murmurs away. I shudder ...
Willows, like bathing women, bend their foreheads and ash-blond
    falling hair towards the pond.

Say, does a snail-horn bode well for the one who
    picks it up?
If you doubt, I will give it to the waters.
How they crinkle, how they billow ... silken ... and still glisten
    coldness.
Beloved, let us still sit here a little, on the only open small
    sunny spot in the reed bed,
And look across to the windows, our windows,
    knotted around by clematis and darker ivy.
How I like this small castle hidden away from the world, enclosed
    in shade!
Also the wall decorations, also the blackened
    gilding, the crumbling Cherubs, the weary
    wreaths of flowers,
Also the moss, hanging off the cracked
    Greek vases.
Also by the gate the mighty lime and its wood-pigeon
    calling again with darkening cooing.
And the elaborately forged lattice ...

Are you going now ... Shall I follow already? Lead me; I
    shiver ... I fear ...
I would like to swim up to the water-lilies the
    yellow glow.

Sieh', der Flausch deiner Brust wuchert algenhaft, und ich
weiß: der Wassermann bist du.
Und ich weiß: unzählige Schätze, Seesilber, Schlämmgold,
häufst du tief in verborgenen Kammern unter dem
Wasser, der Erde.
Wirst du jetzt meine Hände nehmen, mit mir zum Grunde
tauchen, zur Pforte, die ein schwerer, schnauzbärtiger
Wels bewacht?
Soll ich nie Schwester noch Bruder mehr sehn, nicht den
alten Vater mehr, den ich liebe?
Du, ich bebe …
Wenn ich empfinge: mein Kind trüge Schwimmhäute
zwischen Fingern und Zehn, trüge Muscheln und
Wasserlinsen seltsam in immer triefenden Haaren.
Kehr' ans Ufer … Spötter!
Flüsterst du scherzend, ich müßte dir Zwillingsknaben,
Kastor und Polydeukes, gebären, weil ihrer königlichen
Mutter Name mich schmückt?
Glauben denn wir, daß im Schwan ein Göttliches irdischem
Weibe zu nahn vermag? Die liebliche Fabel? —
Ich verstumme … ich log …
Meine kosenden Hände ducken Gefieder, tasten weicheren
Flaum, und weiße, zitternd gebreitete Fittiche schlagen
über mich hin …

Look, the fleece of your chest proliferates like algae, and I
    know: you are the water sprite.
And I know: countless riches, sea-silver, sludge-gold,
    you hoard deep in hidden chambers under the
    water, under the earth.
Will you take my hands now, dive with me to the bottom,
    to the gate guarded by a heavy, moustached
    catfish?
Shall I never see sister or brother again, nor the
    old father any more, whom I love?
You, I tremble …
If I conceived: my child would have webs between
    fingers and toes, would strangely wear mussels and
    water lentils in endlessly dripping hair.
Back to the bank … Mocker!
Are you whispering in jest, that I must bear you twin boys,
    Castor and Pollux, because their royal mother's
    name adorns me?
Do we really believe that a God through a swan can approach
    an earthly woman? The charming fable? —
I fall silent … I lied …
My caressing hands nestle feathers, feel softer
    down, and white quiveringly-spread wings
    beat over me …

Das Opfer

Ihre purpurnen Schuhe kennen den Weg und die Spange um
    ihren Knöchel weiß ihn.
So wandelt sie ohne Willen, gebunden, im Traum.
So wandeln die heißen dunkelnden Augen durch Reihen
    steinerner Flügelkatzen und schwerer bemalter Säulen
    zum Vorhof des Tempels,
Da ein nackter Greis in schmutzigem Lendentuche auf
    winziger Pauke hämmert und endlos sein näselnder
    Singsang fleht.
Die Aussätzige, von wirren Haaren verhangen, reckt
    stöhnend den Arm.
Unfruchtbare seufzen Gebete.
Ein Jüngling steht hoch und steil, unbeweglich, mit breitem
    bronzenen Schwert,
Und ein Wahnsinniger krümmt mit leisem verzückten
    Lachen sich über rosengranitener Schwelle.
Wie sie vorüberstrebt, hascht die Kranke, Verdeckte nach
    ihrem Kleide, den amarantfarbenen Säumen;
Sie aber zieht, die Wolke, an unerreichbaren Abendhimmeln
    dahin.

Dreimal fragt ihre pochende Hand die kupferne Tür, die ihr
    dreimal erwidert.
Ein Priester öffnet.
Sein Bart rinnt, blauer Fluß, über die linnene Bleiche des
    Untergewandes, den Safran des Mantels.
Auf seiner hohen schwarzen Haube spreizt ein silberner
    Vogel sich.
Er gießt Milch in rote Tonschalen, Milch der wachsweißen
    Kuh mit vergoldeten Hörnern,
Trank den heiligen Schlangen,
Die ihre glatten, getuschten Leiber am Boden des
    düsternden Raumes knäueln und wälzen.

The Sacrifice

Her purple shoes know the way and the clasp around
    her ankle understands it.
So she moves without will, bound, in a dream.
So the hot darkening eyes move through rows of
    stony winged cats and solid painted columns
    to the vestibule of the Temple,
Where a naked old man in a filthy loin cloth pounds onto a
    tiny kettle-drum and his nasal sing-song
    pleads endlessly.
The leper, covered with tangled hair, stretches
    the arm groaningly.
Barren ones sigh prayers.
A youth stands tall and straight, immovable, with broad
    bronze sword,
And a demented one with gentle ecstatic
    laughter bends over a rose granite threshold.
As she pushes past, the sick one, the covered one snatches at
    her dress, at the amaranth coloured hems;
However, she, the cloud passes in unattainable evening
    skies.

Three times her knocking hand asks the copper door which
    answers her three times.
A priest opens.
His beard flows, blue river, over the linen pallor of the
    undergarment, the saffron of the cloak.
On his high black hood a silver bird
    displays itself.
He pours milk into red earthen bowls, milk of the wax white
    cow with gilded horns,
Drink for the holy serpents,
Which tangle and writhe their sleek inky bodies on the floor of
    the darkening room.

Und eine größte chrysolithäugige hebt sich und lauscht und
    wiegt den Bauch zu unhörbarem Liede.
Die Frau verneigt sich ihr, schirmt mit dem Finger das Auge
    und küßt der Natter die Stirn. —
Sie schweigt
Und tritt hinaus in den leeren inneren Hof;
Nur perlmutterne Tauben picken Weizenkörner vom
    lauchgrünen Nephrit.
Sie ängsten nicht.
Zwischen bunt beladenen Wänden hält streng und schmal
    eine Ebenholzpforte sich,
Und dreimal rührt die Frau mit elfenbeinernem Stabe das
    Schloß, das ihr Antwort weigert.
Sie bleibt und wartet.

Dort wird sie eingehn.
Unter dem Bilde des Abgotts mit goldenen Krötenschenkeln,
Im Rauche glimmenden Sandelholzes,
Beim Strahlen zuckenden Feuers
Wird der Fremde nahn,
Wird langsam schreiten und seine rechte Hand auf ihre Mitte
    legen als ein Zeichen.
Er wird sie hinführen in den sengenden Kreis
Und ihre Brüste schauen
Und schweigend stark aus glühen Umarmungen Wollust
    schmelzen.
Sie töten …
So ist es ihr vorbestimmt und sie weiß es.

Sie zaudert nicht. Kein Beben zwingt ihre Glieder; sie blickt
    nicht um,
Kennt weder Glück noch Unglück.
Sie füllte sich ganz mit brennender Finsternis, mit dumpf
    erglänzender Demut, die dem Gebote des Scheusals
    dienen, dem goldenen Götzen sterben will. —

And a biggest chrysalis-eyed one raises herself and listens, and
    sways her belly to the inaudible song.
The woman bows to her, shields the eye with the finger
    and kisses the viper's forehead. —
She is silent
And steps out into the empty inner yard;
Only mother-of-pearl doves peck wheat grains from
    the allium-green Nephrite.
They don't fear.
Between colourfully loaded walls an ebony gate maintains itself,
    severe and narrow,
And three times with an ivory crosier the woman touches the
    lock which refuses to answer her.
She remains and waits.

There she will enter.
Under the image of the idol with golden toad thighs,
In the smoke of the glimmering sandalwood,
In the radiance of the flaring fire
The stranger will approach,
Will stride slowly and lay his right hand on her middle
    as a sign.
He will lead her into the scorching circle
And behold her breasts
And silently powerful, smelt voluptuousness out of glowing
    embrace.
Will kill her …
So it is pre-ordained for her and she knows it.

She does not hesitate. No quivering forces her limbs; she
    does not look round,
Knows neither fortune nor misfortune.
She filled herself entirely with burning darkness, with dull
    gleaming humility, which wants to serve the monster's
    decree, which wants to die for the golden idol. —

Doch in ihrem Herzen ist Gott.
Auf ihrem ernsten und schönen Antlitz haftet sein Siegel.
Das aber weiß sie nicht.

Yet God is in her heart.
Her solemn and beautiful countenance bears his seal.
But she does not know that.

Fruchtlos

Die Frauen des Westens tragen den Schleier nicht.
Die Frauen des Ostens legen ihn ab.
Ich möchte mein Antlitz mit dunklem Schleier verhüllen;
Denn es ist nicht schön mehr zu schauen, nicht lieblich
    mehr, denn es ist graulich und rissig wie Steine
    morschen, erkalteten Herdes.
Mein Haar stäubt Asche.

So will ich warten allein in Dämmerung auf schmaler,
    hochlehniger Bank,
So will ich sitzen, da zögernd Nacht um mich sinkt,
Ein schwarzer Schleier.
Ich ziehe ihn um mich und bedeckte mein Gesicht.

Doch meine Augen starren ...

Ich sehe. Ich fühle:
Durch die verschlossene Tür tritt lautlos
Ein Kind.
Das einzige, das mir zubestimmt und das ich nicht geboren.
Nicht geboren um meiner Sünde willen; Gott ist gerecht.
Und ich schweige, und murre nicht, ich trage und berge das
    Haupt, und so darf ich es suchen
Manchen Abend.

Ein Knabe.
Nur dieser eine: zart, stumm und flehend, mit weichen
    düsteren Locken,
Unter bräunlicher Stirn die fremden graugrünen Meeraugen
    dessen, den ich geliebt, den ich immer liebe.
Er fürchtet mich nicht, bebt nicht zurück vor dem
    Schmeicheln der welken Lippen und Hände.

Fruitless

The women of the west don't wear the veil
The women of the east abandon it.
I want to cover my countenance with a dark veil;
Because it is no longer beautiful to behold, not delightful
    anymore, because it is gruesome and cracked like stones
    from a brittle hearth turned cold.
My hair scatters ashes.

So I will wait alone in twilight on narrow,
    high-backed bench,
So I will sit, when night sinks hesitantly around me,
A black veil.
I pull it around me and covered my face.

But my eyes stare …

I see. I feel:
Through the locked door steps silently
A child.
The only one that was meant for me and that I didn't give birth to.
Not born because of my sins; God is just.
And I keep quiet, and don't grumble, I endure and hide the
    head, and thus I may seek for it
Many an evening.

A youth.
Only this one: delicate, mute and pleading, with soft,
    dark locks,
Under brownish forehead the strange grey-green sea-eyes
    of the one whom I loved, whom I always love.
He does not fear me, does not shy from the
    flattering of the faded lips and hands.

Er naht und sein blauer Sammet rührt meinen Arm und seine
    spielenden kleinen Finger greifen nach meiner Seele
Und tun ihr weh.
Zuweilen bringt er mir seine Murmel, die finstere, golden
    geäderte, Tigerauge genannt,
Oder auch eine Blume, blasse Narzisse,
Oder auch eine Muschel, rötlich, mit Warzen; er hebt sie
    sacht an mein Ohr und ich höre dem Rauschen zu.

Einst
Um die Hälfte der Nacht, der Winternacht,
Erwacht' ich und schaute durch Schatten:
Der mich liebte, ruhte auf meinem Lager und schlief.
Sein Atem war Muschelrauschen in Stille.
Ich lauschte.
Und er schlummerte tief, so geborgen in meiner Liebe
Unter Träumen: sie falteten über ihm Flügel, purpurn wie
    Saft des besamten Granatapfels, den wir geteilt.
Friede.
Und ich war glücklich und hob mich und saß, innig betend,
Und neigte wieder das Angesicht und hielt es mit Händen
    und stammelte Dank um Dank.
Aus meinem Blut
Knospete eine Rose ...

Das war die Keimnacht,
Die Segen wollte, Nacht der ungeflüsterten Bitte, doch ich
    empfing dich nicht.
Sieh deine Mutter weinen ...

Auch du wirst sterben.
Morgen werde ich einen Spaten nehmen, unter die
    Schneebeersträucher gehen und dich begraben. —

He approaches, and his blue velvet touches my arm, and his
        little playing fingers take hold of my soul
And hurt it.
Sometimes he brings me his marble, the dark, golden
        veined one, named Tiger-eye,
Or a flower, pale narcissus,
Or a shell, reddish with warts; he lifts it
        gently to my ear, and I listen to the whooshing.

Once
In the middle of the night, the winter night,
I woke and beheld through shadows:
The one who loved me lay on my bed and slept.
His breathing was shell-murmuring in stillness.
I listened.
And he slumbered deeply, so sheltered in my love
Under dreams: they folded wings over him, crimson like
        the juice of seeded pomegranate that we shared.
Peace.
And I was happy and lifted myself and sat fervently praying,
And bowed the countenance again and held it with hands
        And stammered thanks upon thanks.
Out of my blood
Budded a rose ...

That was the seminal night,
Wanting benediction, night of the unwhispered plea, but I
        did not conceive you.
See your mother weep ...

You too will die.
Tomorrow I will take a spade, go under the
        snowberry bushes, and bury you. —

Der Ural

Wenn ich Finsternis packe, verwunden Schroffen
Meine Hand.
Da ist Gebirg, das mit Zacken und Schründen sich aufsteilt
    und bäumt wie eines Drachen Kamm.
Da ist der Ural.
Kette von Nord nach Süd, Scheide von West und Ost, Mauer
    zwischen zwei Erden.
Ich muß die Lampe löschen, daß er werde, daß er von mir
    krieche, riesiges Echsengetüm, in Nacht.
Denn es quillt sein Gestein und sein Gewälde wächst
Aus meiner Seele.
Und der Hauch meines Mundes webt rauchig über dem Schnee
    des Jaman-tau, meines ewigen Gipfels.

Ich sinne.

Plumpe, zottige Bären trollen brummend aus Höhlen,
Wolfsnasen wittern im Bruch,
Braunpelzige Zobelmarder schleichen.
Selbst schuf ich das fiedrig schreckende gelbäugige
    Eulengesicht
Und springendem Quellfluß den großen grausilbernen Fisch
Und schwarzen Forsten schwere flügelknatternde Auerhähne,
Die immer wieder doch meines Felsenadlers goldene
    Kralle schlägt und aufreißt in Lüfte …
Aber die Wurzel großer düstermähniger Tanne stößt in
    Tiefen, drängt augenlos blind unerschöpflichen
    Kammern zu, getürmten, gehäuften Schätzen,
Die da Grün sind: Schlangenhäutiger Serpentin, Otter
    unter den Steinen, und Malachit wie erstarrtes Laub
Und hellerer Chrysopras, den Sonne nicht sehen darf, die
    ihm gierig den Apfelglanz aussaugt und fahlt.

The Urals

When I seize darkness, jagged edges wound
My hand.
There are mountains which rise and buck with spikes
and crevasses like the crest of a dragon.
There are the Urals.
Chain from North to South, division between West and East, wall
between two worlds.
I must put out the lamp, so that it might become, so that it
might crawl away from me, immense lizard-being, in night.
For its rocks swell, and its forests grow
Out of my soul.
And the breath of my mouth weaves smoky over the snow
of the Jaman-tau,[6] my eternal summit.

I muse.

Clumsy, shaggy bears lollop out of caves, growling,
Wolf-noses sniff in the swamp,
Brown furry sable-martens slink.
Myself, I created the shocking feathery yellow-eyed
owl face
And the great grey-silver fish for the leaping flowing source
And the heavy wing-flapping wood grouse for the black forests,
Which, again and again, the golden talons of my rock eagles
smite and rip apart into air ...
But the root of the great dusk-maned pine tree thrusts into
the depths, pushes eyelessly blind towards inexhaustible
chambers, towards stacked, heaped treasures,
Which are green: snake skinned serpentine, adder
under the stones, and malachite like fossilised leaves
And brighter chrysoprase, which must not see the sun that
avariciously sucks and fades its apple splendour.

---

[6] The highest mountain in the Southern Urals is Jaman-Tau (1640 m)

Edelerz flimmert; Rubinkörner locken verstreut die
    Schnäbel unterirdischer hammerköpfiger Vögel.
Mandelsteine reifen, mit buntem Achat gefüllt; Chalcedon
    schwillt traubig,
Und brauner Marmor mit eingesprengten orangenen
    Muscheln
Dämmert …

All das ist schön.

Aber ich habe anderes noch, Widriges, Dumpfes:
Schattenschlünde, da Ungestalt hockt, Halbwesen, das mir
    entschlüpfte, eh' ich ihm Herzschlag gab.
Stumm, erstickt schreit es nach mir, doch mich schaudert;
    ich blicke nicht nieder.
Es harrt der Erlösung …
Einmal vielleicht, einmal
In kalter, sternloser Trübe,
Wenn Winternacht leise pfeift wie ungeheure grauliche Ratte,
Baumstümpfe, faulige Stummelzähne, im Munde der Erde
    kaun,
Flocken gespenstisch Leichentücher erstorbenem Hochmoor
    breiten —
Dann werde ich hingehn
Und, meine Hände auf bebender Brust, mich dem
    Abgrund neigen …

Precious minerals shimmer; scattered ruby seeds lure the
    bills of underground hammer-headed birds.
Almond stones ripen, filled with colourful agate; chalcedony
    swells grape-like,
And brown marble, scattered with orange
    shells,
Dawns …

All of that is beautiful.

But I also have the other, the unfavourable, the lacklustre:
Shadow gullets, where the misshapen one squats, half creature, which
    escaped me before I gave it pulsating life.
Mute, suffocated, it screams for me, but I shudder;
    I do not look down.
It waits for redemption …
Once, maybe once
In cold starless gloominess,
When winter-night whistles softly like a monstrous grey rat,
When tree stumps, rotten stubs of teeth, chew in the mouth
    of the earth,
When flakes spread ghostly shrouds for the dead
    high moor —
Then I will go there,
And my hands on trembling breast,
    bend towards the abyss …

Die Stadt

Sie gingen
Durch den nebelleicht kühlen Wintermorgen, Liebende,
    Hand in Hand.
Erde bröckelte hart, gefrorene Pfütze sprang gläsern unter
    den Sohlen.
Drunten am Uferwege
Saß einer in brauner Sammetjoppe vor seiner Staffelei
Und malte die blattlos hängende Weide.
Kinder pirschten neugierig näher,
Und die Großen hielten für Augenblicke mit ihrem Gange
    ein, tadelten, lobten.
An dem algengrünen, glitschigen Stege
Schwamm ein lecker, verrotteter Kahn.
Drei Schwäne über den Wellen
Bogen die stengelschlanken Hälse, schweigend, entfalteten
    sich, blühten.
Die Frau brach Brot und warf es weit in die Flut.

Unter starrenden Eichen,
Die Äste, schwarz, verrenkt, wie gemarterte Glieder streckten,
Schritten sie an den fröstelnden Rasen, efeuumwucherten
    Pfeilern verschlossener Gärten dahin.
Als sie die lange steinerne Brücke betraten,
Riß Sonne den Nebel von sich wie ein Gewand,
Und die Stadt stieg auf, schräg hinter dem breiten Becken
    des Flusses.
Ineinander, übereinander schoben sich Dächer, schwarzgrau
    glänzend wie Dohlengefieder, einzelne, höhere
    patinagrün; goldene Turmhauben blitzten.
Möwen umkreischten, hungrig flatternde Bettler, das
    Brückengeländer.
Sie waren hinüber

The City

They walked
Through the cool light-misty winter morning, lovers,
    hand in hand.
Earth crumbled hard, frozen puddle burst like glass under
    the soles.
Down there by the river path
Someone, in a brown velvet jacket, sat in front of his easel
And painted the leafless weeping willow.
Children crept inquisitively closer,
And the adults momentarily stopped walking
    criticised, praised.
By the algae-green slippery pier
Floated a leaking, rotted punt.
Three swans over the waves
Curved the stalk-slender necks, mute, unfolded
    themselves, blossomed.
The woman broke bread and threw it far onto the waters.

Under staring oaks
Which stretched their branches, black, contorted like tormented limbs,
They strode past shivering lawns, past ivy, rampant over
    pillars of locked-up gardens.
When they stepped onto the long stony bridge
Sun ripped the mist from itself like a robe,
And the city rose up, oblique behind the broad basin
    of the river.
Into each other, over each other, roofs pushed themselves, black-grey
    shining like jackdaw feathers, some higher ones
    patina green; golden spires flashed.
Seagulls, hungry flapping beggars, screeched around the
    railings of the bridge.
They were across

Und schauten vor mürrisch alltäglichem Hause den Knaben
zu, die ihrem gelben Hund die wunde, blutende Pfote
verbanden.
Frauen mit Marktnetzen, Henkelkörben blickten
vorübereilend die müßigen Fremden knapp und
mißtrauisch an,
Verschwanden hinter den Türen düsterer kleiner murkliger
Läden.

Lauter und stärker, wohlhäbiger, fülliger wurden die Straßen.
Stattliche Gasthöfe luden mit kräftigen Lettern ein;
Rötliche Backsteinmauern standen machtvoll-gewichtig da
gleich Ratsherren alter Zeit mit Puffenwams und Barett
und prunkender Schaube.
Bahnen lärmten fröhlich, bimmelten flink, wie ein
Gassenjunge am Parktor, entwischten.
Männer in dicken, warmen Mänteln beredeten rauchend und
lebhaft schreitend Handel und Wandel,
Und bald fing die Garküche an, ihren Stand mit nahrhaften
Bratgerüchen zu rühmen.
Laden reihte an Laden sich,
Bot zartes, saftiges Fleisch und Wildbret, Fische,
geräucherten Aal und Sprotten,
Bot knusprig braunes längliches Brot, süß, mit Korinthen
gefüllt, und herbes, das mehlüberstäubt oder mit Salz
und Kümmel bestreut war.
Zwischen zwei Kupferbechern duckte ein winziges
chinesisches Teehaus von kirschrot gelacktem Holze
sein geschweiftes vergoldetes Dach.
Doch das Gewölb, da um teures Geld Tränke und Salben
und Pulver gemengt und verabreicht werden,
Wies durchs Fenster den Greis, wie lebend, gebückt
im Sessel,
In wollener Kutte, mit schlohweiß wallendem Bart;
Er schloß die Lider.
Hinter ihm grinste ein langes scheußliches Beingeripp mit
Totenschädels höhnischen Augenhöhlen und Zähnen,

And in front of a sullenly mundane house they watched the boys
    who dressed the wounded bleeding paw of their yellow
    dog.
Women with string bags, baskets with handles, glanced
    terse and mistrustful at the idle strangers, while
    hurriedly passing by,
Vanished behind the doors of small
    dingy shops.

Louder and stronger, more opulent, fulsome became the streets.
Imposing inns invited with potent lettering;
Reddish brick walls stood there powerfully-weighty
    like councillors of olden times with puff jerkin and beret
    and resplendent tabard.
Trams made a happy noise, rang nimbly, like a
    street urchin at the park gate, and scarpered.
Men in thick warm coats discussed doings and dealings, smoking and
    striding energetically,
And soon the Kitchen began to praise its reputation
    with nourishing smells of frying.
Shop sidled up to shop,
Offered tender, juicy meat and game, fish,
    smoked eel and sprats,
Offered crisp, brown longish bread, sweet, stuffed with currants,
    and savoury, dusted with flour or sprinkled
    with salt and caraway.
Between two copper goblets a tiny
    Chinese tea house of cherry-red lacquered wood
    cowered its curved gilded roof.
But the vault, where potions and ointments and powders are mixed
    and prescribed for good money,
Revealed, through the window, the old man, as if alive, stooped
    in the armchair
In a woollen cowl, with a flowing snow-white beard;
He closed the eyelids.
Behind him grinned a tall hideous skeleton with
    skull's mocking eye-sockets and teeth,

Die glitzernde Sense in einer Hand und mit der andern des
    Sinkenden Schulter krallend.
Eine Uhr zeigte Mitternacht.
Da erschrak die Frau und griff nach dem Manne —

Er nickte und lächelte aber;
Denn er sah nichts als ihr finsteres Haar und ihr blasses
    dunkeläugiges Antlitz.

The glittering scythe in one hand, and with the other
    clawing the shoulder of the sinking one.
A clock showed midnight.
The woman took fright and reached for the man —

But he nodded and smiled;
Because he saw nothing but her dark hair and her
    pale dark-eyed countenance.

Kunst

Sie nahm den Silberstift
Und hieß ihn hingehn über die weiße matt glänzende Fläche:
Ihr Land. Er zog
Und schuf Berge.
Kahle Berge, nackte kantig steinerne Gipfelstirnen, über
     Öde sinnend;
Ihre Leiber
Schwanden umhüllt, vergingen hinter dem bleichen Gespinst
Einer Wolke.
So hing das Bild vor dem schwarzen Grunde, und Menschen
     sahen es an.
Und Menschen sprachen:
»Wo ist Duft? Wo ist Saft, gesättigter Schimmer?
Wo das strotzende, kraftvoll springende Grün der Ebenen
Und der Klippe bräunlich verbranntes Rot oder ihr taubes
     graues Düster?
Kein spähender Falke rüttelt, hier flötet kein Hirt.
Nie tönen groß in milderes Abendblau die schön
     geschwungenen Hörner wilder Ziegen.
Farbenlos, wesenlos ist dies, ohne Stimme; es redet zu uns
     nicht.
Kommt weiter.«

Sie aber stand und schwieg.
Klein, unbeachtet stand sie im Haufen, hörte und schwieg.
Nur ihre Schulter zuckte, ihr Blick losch in Tränen.
Und die Wolke, die ihre zeichnende Hand geweht,
Senkte sich und umwallte, hob und trug sie empor
Zum Schrund ihrer kahlen Berge.
Ein Wartender,
Dem zwei grüngoldene Basilisken den Kronreif schlangen,
Stand im Dämmer auf, glomm und neigte sich, sie zu grüßen.

Art

She took the silver pen
And told it to glide over the white mat-glistening surface:
Her land. It drew
And created mountains.
Barren mountains, naked stony-edged summit-brows musing
    over waste land;
Their bodies
Disappeared shrouded, faded behind the pale web
Of a cloud.
Thus hung the image in front of the black ground and People
    looked at it.
And People spoke:
"Where is smell? Where is juice, saturated shimmer?
Where is the strutting, powerfully-leaping green of the plains
And the cliff's brown-burnt red or its dead-
    grey darkening?
No peering falcon hovers, no shepherd flutes here.
The beautifully-curved horns of wild goats never boast in
    milder evening blue.
Colourless, without essence, is this, without voice; it does not speak
    to us.
Let's go."

But she stood and said nothing.
Small, unnoticed, she stood in the crowd, listened and said nothing.
Only her shoulder flinched, her look slaked in tears.
And the cloud which her drawing hand had blown
Lowered itself and enveloped, lifted and carried her up
To the crevasse of her barren mountains.
A Waiting One
For whom two golden-green basilisks plaited the diadem,
Rose up in the dusk, glowed and bowed to greet her.

Lightning Source UK Ltd.
Milton Keynes UK
UKOW050613240612

194979UK00001B/16/P